SERVING HOUSE JOURNAL

Vol. 19

Serving House Journal, Vol. 19

Paperback ISBN: 978-1-947175-79-2

This collection contains works of fiction. Any references to historical events, real people or places are used fictitiously.

Cover art by Claire Bateman

Cover design by Jacob Arms

Printed in the United States
Published by Serving House Books
Lawrence Landing Company
Raleigh, North Carolina 27609
www.servinghousebooks.com

Serving House Books is a proud member of:

Independent Book Publishers Association
and
Community of Literary Magazines and Presses

SERVING HOUSE BOOKS

DEDICATED TO

Thomas E. Kennedy (1944-2021)
Gordon Weaver (1937-2021)
Robert Day (1941-2022)

Dear readers,

This past year I was honored to be handed this great responsibility of managing Serving House Books as the new publisher. With such a strong catalogue of impressive creative works, along with the new projects we're planning, this press has a bright future. We are already doing new things with creative contests and calls for submissions, while also staying true to the original vision of Tom and Walter. I wanted to start by bringing back *Serving House Journal*. This first new volume is brief but to the point and full of reasons to celebrate.

This year we came full circle back to Susan Tekulve who was the author of our first full-length book Savage Pilgrims. We released her first full-length poetry collection in December 2024. *Bodies of Light* is a fantastic collection, so we've already had a strong relaunch into the literary world. Tekulve's book was followed by a collection of short stories by a new Serving House author Eugene Datta. His manuscript was the first to overwhelm the reading committee (and myself) with a sense of literary joy; we jumped on it with an offer and thankfully he accepted. Datta's collection *The Color of Noon* was also published in December 2024. Our first two selections are exclusive works from these first two published works of the new era.

For our fiction selections, we start out with a memorable work from our cofounder Walter Cummins "Missing Venice." The second story "Brooklyn Summer Rain" is from Susan O'Neill who did a new edition of her book *Don't Mean Nothing* with the press in 2010. The third story is from Miriam Polli, whose 2014 novel *In a Vertigo of Silence* we published; her piece is a chapter from her forthcoming historical novel *Rosina* due out in January by Serving House. Finally, our fiction selections conclude with "Artifacts" the title story of our best-selling collection *Artifacts and Other Stories* by Ronna Wineberg.

Our poetry works also return to previously published Serving House authors starting with Claire Bateman, whose two selections come from her 2012 Serving House book *Locals.* Claire is actually our first published author with a chapbook titled *Coronology,* which is also why we celebrate Claire on the front cover with her artwork! Barbara Froman who published *Ghosts and Shadows in 2011 with Serving House* contributed the next poem, showing her versatility. The next poem is from Maria Mazziotti Gillan whose works paired with the photography of Mark Hillringhouse was issued as a special compilation in 2017 titled *Paterson Light and Shadow.* A poem follows by Diana Senechal who is a new Serving House author but a well-established artist with many other publications; her poetry collection *Solo Concert* will be released in January 2025. Rota Signorelli-Pappas returns with a poem from her forthcoming Serving House book *The Chameleon,* which will be her third book with the press. And two poems from another returning SHB author J.R. Solonche concludes our poetry selections; his next collection *Barren Road* is set for release in 2025 too!

At the conclusion of this collection is an abridged version of my interview with cofounder Walter Cummins. We had a great long talk about his career and the founding of the press. You can listen to the whole interview on my podcast *The Purpose Tree,* where I interview many other writers and artists. In fact, soon I'll have a whole Serving House series.

This collection is a celebration of Serving House authors, old and new. We'll continue to celebrate their works as we grow the family of artists and welcome in new authors in 2025.

Wishing you well in the new year,
Bill,

William K. Lawrence
Publisher, Serving House Books

CONTENTS

Exclusives

Fiction

Poetry

Interview

Contributor's Notes

SUSAN TEKULVE

For the Spiders

After Edward Hirsch

September, the air no longer a hairshirt
of heat and mosquitoes, I want to praise spiders
whose webs cinch muscadine vines to my cabin's side,

hang like iridescent handkerchiefs
around junipers and stone pines whose silvery needles
hush the buck crashing the understory.

I love how spiders are willing to stay up all night
like lonely old women mending and rearranging
summer's last belongings

tossing webbed antimacassars across soft backs
of hydrangeas whose final blooms
dim into candelabra white.

And always a spider's solid body replaces
the dissolving moon outside my window at dawn:
That's why I want to say: Our souls are silken trails of light

following a black creek running
through a moonlit pasture, its banks
brimming with goldenrod and aster

below solid cattle leaning
in sleep, warming sides against warm sides
holding each other upright, together.

We have to trust our souls will hold our bodies, fallen
in sleep, as a spider's web holds fallen beech
and oak leaves unready to touch the ground.

We have to trust our bodies will awaken whole,
together and solid as spiders
after a night of mending the earth.

From the collection *Bodies of Light* (2024)

EUGENE DATTA

The Color of Noon

The sunlight on the window ledge is the color of noon. The house is unusually quiet.

"Jane?" he calls softly, still lying in bed. No response. "Are you there?"

In the lane bellow, the tinkling of a rickshaw-wallah's bell comes closer. It stops near the door; the sound of rickshaw handles being lowered to the ground. *Is that her?* Jane works the night shift at a local nursing home. She comes home by nine every morning, and never goes out again until five thirty.

The footsteps stop in front of their door, then resume climbing. It's Mrs. Aratoon; she lives upstairs. Her old dog whimpers, barks weakly, then whimpers again.

It's twelve seventeen by the clock on his bedside table. Not yet time for Jane's afternoon nap. Not time for his mother to be back, either. She teaches at a primary school in the neighborhood, and comes home after lunch. Two pigeons fly back to their perch outside the window and start fighting.

"Jane?" he calls more loudly. Still no response. *Thank God,* he thinks. He's glad no one is at home.

The head! It feels like a lump of sore clay. *It must be the booze.* Lying on his back, he presses it on both sides with the heel of his palms. He imagines kneading it like a potter kneads his clay, or the way Jane kneads her dough when she makes chapati. The throbbing stops for a moment, then returns as soon as he eases the pressure. Mrs. Aratoon's dog begins to whimper again. *She'll die one of these days, poor dog. Poor, sweet dog!* He doesn't remember her name anymore. He used to like playing with her when both of them were younger. He never wanted to have one himself. *Not after Lucky.* Losing her was terrible. It was like in that Harold Robbins story where the dog dies and the boy says he hates dogs because they die. Something like that. He hated losing Lucky.

The pigeons go on fighting. He imagines them using words. He imagines them screaming at each other using the nastiest of words he knows. His stock of cuss words surprises him. He wonders where he learned all these words, all these "unholy" words, as his mother calls them.

He gets up from bed and shuffles to the bathroom. Switching on the light, he stands in front of the mirror. His bladder hurts, but he cannot take his eyes off the face, the one staring at him through the dust-covered, spotted glass under the dim, yellow light.

"Winfred," it whispers. "Winfred..."

"Yes!" he says.

"You killed a man," the face says.

It was around eleven at night last night. They were on their way out of Ghalib Bar on Elliot Road. *Too many drinks, as always.* Ismail and Shibu had already got into the car, and Win was waiting for Munna to come out of the toilet. He heard a noise inside and knew something was wrong. But before he could get there, the toilet door burst open. It was Munna. He had a bag in his hand, which wasn't his. "Let's get out of here," he said and made for the door. "Quick!" Munna hissed. One of the waiters had gone into the toilet in the meantime; he came out and screamed, "Stop that man, he's killed someone!"

Munna was out of the bar, and Win was almost near the door when this fat man tumbled out of a booth. He stood blocking Win's path. "Hold it there," the man slurred, spreading out his arms like a kabaddi player. A big man with a soft, melon-like face. Win had to get him out of the way before the waiters could reach him. His whole body was shaking. He reached for the switchblade knife he always carried in his pocket. He wanted to take it out and hold it in front of him, so that the bugger wouldn't get close. But he did. He lunged forward, *the drunk bastard!* He threw himself at Win just as Win's hand was stretching out with the knife pointed toward him. He dropped the knife as soon as he felt it had touched the man's body—which part he couldn't tell. The man let out a strange noise, and collapsed to the floor. Win leaped over his body and ran out.

Ismail had already started the car. Munna pushed open the rear door. "Get in," he shouted. "Fast!"

Within moments, they were on Rafi Ahmed Kidwai Road. Ismail made a sharp right turn just as the traffic lights changed to red.

Win was relieved he was sitting in Ismail's car instead of being pinned down by the waiters at Ghalib. Or beaten up. He cursed himself for touching the knife. *Why didn't he just push the bugger out of the way?* He was so unsteady a single push would have done the job. *But, no, he had to take out the fucking knife!* "This knife will get you into trouble one day," Jane had told him many times. Why didn't he listen to her and stop carrying the damn thing? He remembered the man he'd bought it from; he remembered that shriveled-raisin face of his. Another one of those Sudder Street tourists. He said he was a retired sailor from Australia. "I have no use for this beauty anymore," he'd said about the knife. "I need some cash for my trip to the hills." Win remembered that scratchy voice of his. It sounded like the man had gargled with pieces of glass, and some were still stuck in his throat. He remembered the look on his face as he was counting the money Win had just given him. He'd borrowed it from Jane, promising to return it soon, which he never did. *What a mistake the whole thing was!*

Ismail was driving like crazy. His father's old Padmini whined and sputtered trying to run as fast as it could. He's the only one in the gang who even knows how to drive—he's from that type of family. The type that owns cars, shops, tanneries, and who knows what else. The rest of them cannot even dream about such things.

Inside the car, silence. Win had no idea where they were going. "Where are we going?" he finally asked.

"To fucking hell!" Ismail barked. "I keep telling you guys not to drink so much and get into bawals!"

"It had nothing to do with drinking." Munna tried to sound calm. "I just hit the bugger in the face. It knocked him out, but he'll be okay. If you knew how he screwed my life you'd be surprised I didn't break his neck today."

"*Screwed your life!*" Ismail hissed. "Now wait and see how *this* screws your life. And ours too! Who knows if there wasn't an off-duty *mamu* sitting there and watching your drama? We can all end up in Lal Bazar because of you! And you stole the guy's bag?"

"At least that!" Munna said.

"And Win?" Ismail tilted his head at the window.

Win was directly behind him, trapped in the smell of tanned leather that always hangs around him. Everything that belongs to Ismail carries that smell; it goes wherever he goes. The smell reminded Win of Ismail's house, the godown full of leather, rolls and rolls of it everywhere.

"This fat bugger sitting near the door got in the way," he said.

"And?"

"I think I...nicked him." Win couldn't believe he said that.

"The chap with curly hair and glasses? Alone, right?"

"Yeah. In a black T-shirt."

"Fuck!" Ismail screamed. "I think I *know* the man!"

They reached the Eden Gardens. Ismail slowed the car. No one spoke. They sat still, looking over their shoulders from time to time to see if they were being followed. The street was flooded with neon light. The Maidan club tents, the rickety wooden galleries and the stadium on the other side loomed in the still night like monsters about to wake from their sleep.

They circled the area, drove up and down Strand Road, and crossed the Howrah Bridge several times. After about an hour, Ismail stopped the car in front of a godown in Bara Bazar. He'd spotted a little space between two big trucks loaded with goods. He parked the car there, and turned off the engine. It stopped with a tired, raspy sigh. The two gigantic vehicles hid the car from streetlight, which made Win feel safer than when they were driving.

Ismail lit a cigarette and took a long drag. "He looked familiar," he said. "But not sure why. Maybe I've seen him with Baba. Maybe one of his customers." He took a few more drags, then passed the cigarette to Shibu. It was obvious who he was talking about—not Munna's man, but Win's.

A fresh wave of anxiety crashed on Win's chest. The jolt made his heart start to race again. He started to think, once again, about how easily he could have got out of that place without hurting the man. All he needed to do was just push the guy out of the way. Just one big shove, and he would've been back down in his booth. Win would've been inside the car by the time he could get himself on his feet again. The man was too drunk to be any real threat, but he was too scared to see it at the time. *Too fucking scared!* He clenched his jaw. A cold sweat trickled down his body where the shirt didn't touch his skin.

It was past one in the morning when Win got out of the car on S.N. Banerjee Road. He wanted to walk, he told Ismail.

Smith Lane was quiet. Close to their house, it was darker than usual; at least one streetlight wasn't working. And no one seemed to be awake except Bahadur, the Nepali night watchman. "Hello, Vinshab, everything okay?" he called out the way he always does, as if there's always a chance something is not okay. *But didn't he sound slightly different? Like there was a reason why he was asking him if everything was alright?* Win raised his hand in reply and quickly slipped into the passage leading to the main door. He unlocked the door, stepped in and pushed the door gently shut. The stairwell was pitch-dark, but he didn't switch on the lights. He was used to coming home late and feeling his way up six flights of wooden stairs to get to their flat.

He stood in front of the door for a few moments, the smaller of the two keys held between his thumb and forefinger. He eased it into the lock and turned it as softly as he could. He pushed the door just enough to let himself in quietly. Inside, the darkness was alive with the sound of his mother's snores. He filled his lungs with the warm, soothing scent of home—the air heavy with the smell of food, talcum powder and soap. The nightmare at Ghalib seemed distant and unreal, as if it *was* a real nightmare, and he'd just woken up from it.

He took off the shoes and tiptoed into his room. As he lay down on the bed, he felt himself sinking into a darkness that spun like a whirlpool.

"You killed a man," the face in the mirror says again.

No, wait! It was probably just a nick on his chest. Maybe a small gash. It couldn't kill a big man like him. No way! I didn't push the knife. Maybe they took him where Jane works. Maybe that's why...she isn't home yet? God!

Somebody is at the door. He's sure he heard a knock—a light one, the way Shibu does it. Everyone in the gang has a different way of knocking the door, and Shibu does it only once and so lightly you can miss it sometimes. But Win is sure he heard it.

"Come in," he says to Shibu, opening the door, then runs back to the bathroom to pee.

"Hurry up," Shibu says.

"Okay, tell me," Win says, flushing the toilet and washing his hands. "What happened?"

"We're fucked."

Shibu takes out a folded sheet of newspaper from his pocket and hands it to Win. "Take a look."

Win spreads the paper on the table, smoothing it hurriedly with both palms. "Where is it?"

"At the bottom. Left side. That one there. He's in the ICU. The police are looking for us."

"It says local medical center," Win says, reading across a patch where the paper has soaked up the dampness from his fingers. "Doesn't say exactly where. I have a feeling they took him where my sister works. That's the only hospital in that area. Listen, I'm going to get out of here now."

"Where are you going?"

"No idea. Maybe to a friend's place in Howrah. And stay there for a few days. I don't know."

Win is surprised he said Howrah. The friend who lives there is Gopi Nath Rai, someone he hasn't seen in a long time—at least two or three years. They used to be close in school, then life took them in different directions. The last time they met, Gopi talked about his job in the railways, and his wedding, which was around the corner. "You have to come," Gopi had said. He'd sent an invitation too, but Win didn't go. He sent a card with an apology and a false excuse. He doesn't remember what he'd said about why he couldn't come, but the real reason was, he didn't want to embarrass himself. They belonged in different places in life—Gopi had made it, and he...well, he did the exact opposite of what his name means. His pet name, that is—the shorter version of his real name. *He hates it!* Every time he hears someone say it (except his mother and Jane, and his friends), it sounds like they're making fun of him. Like, hidden under the sound of Win is its opposite meaning. Like, if they could, they'd call him Lose instead—*Hey, Lose!* Or even better,

Loser! Showing up at Gopi's wedding would've made that obvious—the difference between the two of them, their places in life. And the ridiculous falseness of his name.

Shibu has left. Of course, he wouldn't go to Gopi's! *And stay there for a few days?* What was he thinking?

The pigeons are at it again. He can hear them just as clearly from near the table, which is in front of the kitchen, between the bathroom and the two bedrooms. A narrow table covered with a sheet of rose printed plastic and three chairs. This is where they eat, watched by his black & white father and colored Jesus. Win stands there for a few more minutes, trying to think through things. Things he needs to do now—decide where he's going to go, and for how long.

The sound of footsteps on the stairs makes his thoughts stop. He rushes back into his room and waits near the door, a hand on the door knob. *What if it's Jane?* What if it's his mother? *Or the police?* Should he close the door? He can hear his heart thumping.

As the footsteps come closer, they sound like Mr. Aratoon's. The sound of both feet landing on the same step, two thuds close to each other. But the man has been dead for years. Maybe a brother of his? *But he didn't have a brother!* Maybe a relative then? Or a friend? Or a *fucking* ghost? He's heard his mother talk about hearing ghostly footsteps in the house. Who knows! Win is glad it's not either her or Jane, or anyone looking for him. He closes the door and pulls out his kitbag from the top of his almirah. He gives it a shake to get rid of the dust, then quickly fills it with a pair of jeans, two shirts, underwear, and socks, all of them unwashed, giving off a musty smell. He realizes he didn't change out of his clothes last night, so he's ready. *Ready to run away from home.*

A shiver runs down his spine. He's never had to even *think* of doing such a thing before. His hands and legs begin to feel unsure, as if he's about to lose control over them. He's been in trouble before, but nothing ever as serious as this. He sneezes—once, twice, three times, four times. It's the dust from the bag.

On his way out, he slips into the bedroom his mother shares with Jane. Both windows in the room are closed, the smell of Ponds in the stale air, the talcum powder his mother uses. Switching on the light, he walks to Jane's bed and lifts the mattress. She keeps all her money there in a plastic bag. He takes out a hundred-rupee note and a few ten-rupee ones and drops the mattress. Then lifts it again to put two ten-rupee notes back in the bag. He's left with three more, plus the hundred, which is enough. It's all *her* money after all—he shouldn't have touched it in the first place. But he did, as he always does, and never returns any of it. Like the amount he'd borrowed to buy that *fucking knife*. He'd *borrowed* it, promising he was going to give it back, but didn't. He steps out of the flat with a stab of guilt, and pulls the door shut.

"Where are you going?" Jane says, panting. She's on the landing below, her left hand gripping the banister.

The last thing Win wanted was to run into his sister now. "To Gopi's house," he says hastily.

"Gopi?" Jane frowns.

"Gopi Nath, you know, my—"

"How come? You haven't seen him in years!"

"I saw him yesterday."

"Why are you taking the bag?"

"He said, bring a change of clothes. I want you to meet a friend, he said. A businessman, who's looking for people. He said, maybe—"

"When will you be back?"

"Tomorrow." He climbs down the stairs, relieved he didn't have to cook up more lies to more questions.

"Bye," he says, walking past her.

"Bye," Jane says and begins to trudge up the stairs.

She looks weak and old, almost like their mother. Win feels sad. *Poor Jane!* She's been working like a dog ever since their father died. Couldn't finish college, and took a nursing job so that there was food on the table and money for her brother's school. That was twelve years ago. Now she's thirty-four—*only nine years older than him*—but climbs stairs like someone twice her age. Who knows how long she'll last if things go on like this! Why didn't he think about all this before? Why didn't he...? *Too late, too late now!*

"Jane?" he calls from the landing below. He wants to ask why she was so late today. Was she held up at work for some emergency? Did something come up last night? "Where's Mum?"

"Gone to see Reverend Simon," she says, unlocking the door. "Should be back in an hour."

"Okay, and...um...I took some dough." He leans on the banister, craning his neck. "Hundred thirty."

"Okay."

"Thanks." Win runs down the stairs.

Shibu said Ismail had sent him with that newspaper page. He didn't have to tell Win that; it was obvious. Shibu couldn't have found that report himself. He doesn't read newspapers. And in English? *No way!* He and Munna—they'd never pick up a paper even out of curiosity, unless there's a picture of a Bollywood goddess there. They just listen to the radio, those two. Always glued to their pocket-sized transistor sets, listening to film songs. With him, it's a different story. In his family, reading The Statesman is like going to church. You *cannot* not do it. Win is the only one who doesn't. He doesn't read the paper and he doesn't go to church. He thinks it makes him a bit like Ismail, who smells of leather all the time but doesn't eat meat. Not even chicken. *Crazy!* But Win thinks it's also special—it's one of the many things he likes about the man. Coming from his background, he shouldn't be hanging around with them. But he does. Not only that, he's extremely protective of them, almost like a big brother. Who pays for all the grub and booze when they go somewhere? *Ismail, of course.* He just doesn't like it when they get drunk and things happen. Like last night.

He gets off the tram in Dharmatala. The afternoon sun is beating down on the chaos and noise of trams, buses, taxis, cars and pedestrians. The smell of street food reminds him of his empty stomach. He hasn't had a morsel since Ghalib. He hears the conductor of a minibus screaming *Howrah, Howrah, Howrah, Howrah* and begins to push his way through the crowd to get to the bus. It starts to move, and he breaks into a run. Picking up speed, he catches up to it and grabs hold of the handlebar, while still running. The conductor makes room for him on the footboard and helps him up. He's boarded running buses like this all his life, but doesn't like doing it. He's seen things happen in front of him—people losing their grip on the handlebar and slipping off the footboard, getting close to being run over. Every time he gets on a bus like this, he fears the same thing happening to him.

The bus is not crowded, although most of the seats are occupied. He finds one at the back and slumps down on it, his heart thumping.

"Ticket?" the conductor holds out his hand.

"Howrah station." Win hands him a ten-rupee note, wondering why he said that. *Why did he even board this bus?* He's not going to Gopi's house! He wonders if his mother is back home yet. He imagines the two of them talking—his mother and Jane:

Where's Win?

He's gone to Gopi Nath's house.

Who?

Gopi Nath Rai, Mum. His friend from St James'. Remember?

No, I don't.

Said Gopi invited him to meet a friend for a job or something.

A lie!

How's Father Simon?

Please tell your darling brother to get a real job or get out of this house. Okay? Enough is enough!

I will, Mum. Tell me about Father now. Is he alright?

A bit better. But you know how these people are, Maria and her husband. They just don't know how to nurse people properly. Low-caste Anglos! Not educated enough, that's the problem.

Win can feel the corners of his mouth stretching into a thin smile. The bus is stuck in a traffic jam in Bara Bazar. Looking out of the window he recognizes the place where they'd parked between the trucks last night. He remembers the sense of relief he'd felt when Ismail squeezed the car into that dark spot and turned off the engine. How *safe* it felt to be there for a few moments, hidden from light! Now the place is filled with harsh sunlight, street vendors and noise.

He told Shibu to tell Ismail he'd try to call tonight. "If I can't do it tonight, tell him I'll do it tomorrow," he said. "Tell him I won't be at home. I'll be in Howrah."

Howrah! That's where he's headed now, but he has no idea why. He thinks of the knife. *I have no use for this beauty anymore....* He remembers the man's name—*Kevin Hogg*. Who knows what's happened to the knife. Maybe the police took it for investigation. Or maybe in all that confusion, people forgot about it and it's still lying there on the floor. In a dark corner, where the sweeper's broom doesn't reach, a rat or two licking at the dried blood on the blade. And who knows where Kevin Hogg is! Did he ever use Win's money—*Jane's* money—to go to the hills?

Boats. He can see several of them. Small fishing boats with open cabins and tarpaulin-covered roofs. The bus is almost near the middle of the bridge, and is hardly moving because of another jam. The woman next to him had the window seat—she left before the bus got on the bridge. Win is glad she did.

He loves the way the river looks. He could sit there just like that and keep looking at the water, and its changing colors—muddy gold, green, gray, silver. There's a bit of cloud in the sky, a warm haze hanging in the air. The breeze on his face feels damp. He stares at the bright blue roof of a tiny boat as it edges closer to the bank. Below him, a bigger one makes its way from under the bridge down the middle of the river. A passenger boat.

A passenger boat! He was once on a boat like that, going in the same direction—a long time ago, almost thirteen years. They were going to the botanical gardens. The Aratoons were there, too. It was a January day, just after their Christmas—the 5th or the 6th of January, Win doesn't remember exactly when. Christmas in January is a strange idea anyway, but that's when the Aratoons celebrated it, and invited his family every year. His father loved drinking rum with Mr. Aratoon, who worked at the Armenian College. He said he was from Iran, and had come to Calcutta as a small boy. He said he'd been to many places in the world, but loved Calcutta the most. This is where I want to die, he said. And he did.

Why is he thinking about it now? He wonders if it's because of the footsteps he heard in the morning. Father Simon was also with them on the boat, and a few other people. His father never liked the man much, Father Simon. Jane said it was because he thought Father flirted with Mum. "Not true, of course," she said. Win had no clue. He just didn't like the funny way Father pronounced his mother's name, as if it was a Bengali name—*Maargareet!*

By next Christmas, their father was gone. The day was 11th November, 1983. And life changed forever.

The bus has started to move again. He can still make out that passenger boat in the crowd of boats in the distance. A thicker crowd of pedestrians at the end of the bridge. He'd have to do it someday, he thinks, cross the bridge on foot and see how it feels. Maybe stand in the middle for some time and look down. The thought sends a shiver down his spine. Suddenly, a rat's twitching nose and whiskers, and its hungry eyes, fill his field of vision—like a closeup on a movie screen, larger than life, gigantic, stretching across everything he can see. The eyes, the twitching nose and whiskers, and crusted blood.

The bus is nearing its stop. Everyone has stood up; Win also gets up from his seat. He tries to get rid of the image, but cannot. The noise that came out of the man's mouth when he collapsed to the floor—Win can hear it through all the honking of the buses, trucks, and taxis. *How is he now?* He was in the ICU—what if he never comes out? *What if he has children at home?*

Win finds himself in the middle of a crowd rushing toward the entrance to the station. He doesn't have a train to catch, but he walks hurriedly to keep himself from getting in the way of people. Although he doesn't have a destination, he feels like he's one of them. He feels like he's part of the crowd—like a cell in a body, like a drop in a river—part of it in a way that makes him completely unknown. And hidden.

A nudge on his shoulder wakes Win. A face with a long, white beard and a big yellow turban with things written on it. A sadhu. The same one he'd sat down next to on the steps going up to the ticket counters.

He'd called Ismail's number twice from the phone booth inside, and both times it was his father, so Win had hung up without saying a word. And he wanted to talk to Jane—he wanted to ask her about the man, but it was still too early for her to be at work, so he had no choice but to wait. Back outside, he'd found a bit of space on the steps at the entrance. The sadhu was sitting there with a cloth sack, a plastic bag and a walking stick. He pulled those things closer to himself and made more room for Win, inviting him to sit down. A family was sitting on the other side. He remembered thanking the man, and feeling glad there was a pillar behind him to rest his back against.

He has no idea how long he slept, but the sun has set. The family has left; there are other people sitting there now. The sadhu is still there, his face right in front of Win's. He's smiling, his right hand holding a paper plate full of puris and curry, steam rising from them. The smell makes Win feel like...if he doesn't take the plate himself within a moment or two, his stomach was going to grow an arm of its own and send it up through his chest and throat, and shoot it out of his mouth to snatch it from the sadhu's hand.

"Thank you," Win says weakly, taking the plate. "Shukriya!" He keeps holding it in front of him, staring at the man's face in disbelief.

The sadhu smiles and motions him to start eating.

WALTER CUMMINS

Missing Venice

A few minutes out of Padua, David dozed into a nightmare that they had missed Venice and, after hours of barely creeping, were suddenly hurtling toward the Adriatic. He felt himself grabbing at suitcases, struggling with the compartment door, desperate to jump from the train and pull Virginia after him, certain that if they did not escape at once, they would plummet into oblivion.

But at a metallic shriek he opened his eyes to iron pipe intestines, the thumping percussion of factories, smokestack fires that seared the darkness. The train lay at a dead stop in Mestre, stalled, as if it would never cross the last kilometers to Venice.

And it wasn't Virginia beside him despite all their months of anticipation, but Donny instead, his son, an oversized fourteen-year-old slouched on the seat, scowling at the flames in the window, kicking unlaced sneakers against a metal panel. The boy hadn't said a word the entire thirteen hours of the trip, through the excruciating pace, the endless delays. He didn't speak; he didn't read; he didn't even listen to his iPod; he just shoved hands deep into his pockets and oozed hostility.

But Maria hadn't shut up since they left the Stazione Termini in Rome. Plump and pockmarked, her shape reminded David of a miniature Donny, though she was a woman in her thirties, an absolute stranger until the middle of that day.

Heavy-lidded, David rubbed hard at his face, fighting off sleep. Maria grinned at his return to consciousness without a hitch in the story she was droning to his son, even though the boy gave no sign of paying attention, something about panic in Tangier, her passport sliding down behind her suitcase lining.

She had stumbled into the compartment, hours ago, just as the train was building momentum to leave Rome, huffing, grinning, baggage spewing from under her arms, off her shoulders.

The trip had begun extremely late, David fuming in his confusion, Donny lagging like dead weight. They stood on a platform for hours, David peering down the empty track, pacing among the heaped suitcases trying to get someone in the crowd of shrugging Italians to explain what had happened to the 8 a.m. Venice express, while Donny muttered curses and stuffed his mouth with candy bars. At 11 a train appeared, and David scrambled aboard, dragging his baggage and his son after him, only to sit for another hour until the creaking start and Maria's breathless arrival.

She was the one to tell them about the one-day railway workers' strike. "We're all victims of a slowdown": the first words out of her mouth, then a non-stop rush, all the time the train inched over countryside, in and out of cities, across a barren brown landscape. Despite her chatter, David sensed that she was as miserable as the boy, her animation a desperate thrashing against a flood of gloom. All day he had felt the compartment sinking, as if the two of them were pulling him under.

To save himself, he gripped the armrest, imagined he was holding Virginia's hand, stroking the soft flesh, blood surging at her warmth. His fantasy of their being alone in a compartment, reaching over to draw a darkening shade and touching his lips to a smooth tanned shoulder. His wife at last, his new life finally begun. For months they had dreamed of being dazzled by the sunset on the Grand

Canal, never considering that they could be an ocean apart, her tickets transferred to a son he barely knew.

"We're in Mestre," Maria said as David blinked his way back to comprehension. "It has a population of 75,000 and manufactures chemicals and heavy metals." Her head was a guidebook. "Pollution from Mestre is a serious problem for Venice. It's in the air, eating into the stucco."

David sighed, long and deep, almost a groan. The last thing he needed on this train was a pathetic lab technician from Santiago compelled to render every detail of every place she had visited during a two-month round-the-world once-in-a-lifetime holiday: the goiter of the woman who rented rooms in Macao, the cockroach found in a cafeteria meal on the Boul' Mich'. Short, squat, fat-faced. He couldn't imagine any man fantasizing about her in a locked compartment.

While David watched his son's eyelids droop and his head slump against the seatback, Maria renewed her outrage about the price of single rooms. "Some hotels charge me for a double even though I only use one bed. Can you believe that?" Her English jarred, with long vowels and trilled r's.

"It must be a problem travelling alone." David swallowed a yawn.

"I live alone. I'm alone most of the time."

The train stirred with a vibration that sent a tremor through the compartment. In his chest David felt the engine strain to break the inertia. He grunted as they lurched forward. Donny turned his face into the cushion and smacked a fist against the metal wall.

"Your son is exhausted," Maria said, then asked, "Do you have other children?" one of the rare moments she did not talk about herself.

David shook his head.

"Will his mother be waiting for you in Venice?"

"His mother is having a baby."

Her mouth dropped.

"His mother is not my wife. Not now. Not for years." David glanced at Donny to see if he was listening, but the boy had an arm around his head, fingers twisted in the hacked ends of a haircut he had given himself.

"I'm married to someone else now." David summoned up a picture of Virginia, soft and slim, lovely in summer dresses. It gave him great pleasure just to watch her move. But he couldn't shut out the memory of the anger that twisted her face: "The reservations are paid for. Nonrefundable. He's your son. Just take him and go."

"And she's in Venice," Maria said, half statement, half question.

"She's back home too."

Maria knotted her brow.

"Look," he said, exasperated. "It's not a big deal. His mother asked me to watch after him for while. She's going to have to adjust to a baby. It's a tough time for everybody."

It had been hell, a night of phones ringing long past midnight, Lucy ranting long distance, Virginia weeping bitterly in the living room, irate women in both his ears. "You bailed out ten years ago," Lucy kept screaming. "Now you see him once a year and stuff him with ice cream. He's infantile. He destroys things. He wants to ruin my marriage. My life! He says he hates my baby! I want him out of here!"

All this three days before their flight, Virginia's suitcase spread open in the guest room, half packed with new clothes, guidebooks and brochures scattered across the carpet. And now beside him a son from half a continent away materialized at an airport gate, off one plane and hauled onto another, a sloppy kid with a smeared chin in a filthy outgrown sweatsuit. Instead of a greeting, he had glared at David and said, "The bitch can shove that baby back where it came from."

"It's nice that you're such a good father," Maria said, and the train lurched.

Finally, at 1:17 a.m. on the station clock, they arrived in Venice. David stirred himself to unfold two chrome luggage carts and strap down suitcases. Maria collected an assortment of canvas bags. Every time she grabbed one, she seemed to drop another. When David offered help, she grinned thanks and let him pick up after her.

For weeks he had anticipated sharing Virginia's awed reaction to discovering Venice. He deliberately had planned their schedule to arrive in early evening in time to change, stroll to an outdoor meal in the Piazza San Marco, and await the sunset. Now it was the middle of the night, Maria squealing at Donny to catch her umbrella.

They emerged from the station into a grey night under a cloud-covered quarter moon. The area was dingy, a row of tiny hotels with faint signs and loiterers slouching in the shadows. They had to wait for a vaporetto in a white shed bobbing at the water's edge. David rolled the two suitcases down a wooden walkway, Maria's heaviest duffle bag over his shoulder. Donny sank onto one of the slat benches, eyes puffed with fatigue.

Whichever direction David looked, up or down the canal, the view was drab, except for the small gold-domed church directly across a slice of water. Maria, seated beside him on the bench, already had her green Michelin guide open. "Fondamente Saint Simeon Piccolo," she said. "There are 190 churches in Venice, nearly all interesting. But I can't find any details about this one." Under a weak bulb she squinted at the page with disappointment.

Aside from two grizzle-faced vaporetto employees smoking cigarettes down to their fingertips, the only others in the waiting shed were three young people, a muscular male in a black turtleneck and faded overalls and two women, one curly headed and round, the other tall and dark, with pitch black hair, drawn cheeks, and stark facial bones. She wore a tank top, long dark legs emerging from cutoff shorts. The night was chilly enough for David to button his sweater. But she did not shiver once.

All three were either drunk or stoned, with arms wrapped around each other, breaking out into snatches of songs, their speech chanted in a language he had trouble placing. It might have been Italian, but with harsh Germanic intonations. The dark woman's loud hoarse voice dominated, as she orchestrated each sound with an angular hand gesture. Every minute or so, at her lead, the three wailed, "Oh, mama!"

Maria grinned at their antics, nudged Donny to make him look, as if the three were putting on a show just for them. But he turned away and spit at the water. David imagined the male suddenly stomping across the planks and knocking Donny into the canal, the boy flailing in a ridiculous splash, then sinking like a stone. A shadow fell across the man's face like a scar, and David swallowed.

When the plump woman gave her the edge of a smile, Maria took that as an excuse to approach and admire the jagged bronze pendant the dark woman wore against her breastbone. The three stared blankly at her English. She tried again in Spanish. After a silence, when the smoking workers halted their conversation to stare, the dark woman glared and did a jerky, arm-flapping dance step that forced Maria backwards. She slunk to the bench and looked to David for solace. But he pretended he had not seen a thing. He caught Donny glancing at him, face screwed in a smirk.

It was another ten minutes before the vaporetto came. By then Maria had located the stop for David's hotel, Campo Santa Maria del Giglio, in her guidebook. His travel agent had made reservations at what she called "a congenial but inexpensive little place" called the Villa Giorgione. He and Virginia had saved for a year; then Lucy's lawyer sent the bill for Donny's therapy, and Virginia had urged him to cancel. But David had insisted that they owed this trip to themselves; he wasn't going to let the son of a failed marriage ruin their future. And now on a chill night at the fringe of Venice he could taste the folly of his decision.

David loaded Maria's suitcases on board and gave her his hand as she stepped down onto the deck. Donny waved off his help. The three young people, without luggage, waited until the boat started to pull away and jumped on with screaming leaps. Maria shrank against David each time a pair of feet pounded the deck.

When the boat began to move, churning out a white wake on the empty canal, she was smiling again, guessing the names of the palaces on the water's edge as if she had memorized the map. Palazzo Grimani, Palazzo Rezzonio, Palazzo Pesaro.

David saw only facades and doorways, silhouettes of roofs and domes, low grey shapes of moored motor launches. He turned and realized that Donny had slipped inside the cabin and collapsed onto a bench, eyes closed, mouth open, chin bouncing against his chest with the vibrations of the boat.

Maria startled him with a nudge and a question. "What is your boy's mother's name?"

"Lucy." It felt odd to be speaking that name here, on a canal in Venice.

"Why did you leave her?"

"I didn't love her."

Her face took on its blank expression. “Is love so important?”

David squeezed his hands around the chill railing. “You wouldn't understand.”

“And the boy?”

“He was a baby then.”

“What is he now?”

“Listen! I didn't make him this way. He lives with his mother.”

Maria looked toward the cabin and gasped. The three young people were hovering over Donny, rising on tiptoes, wriggling fingers. David couldn't hear over the engine noise, but he thought they were chanting.

When he rushed inside, they sprawled across the bench on the other side, arms folded and glaring. He shook Donny; the boy wouldn't open his eyes. “You okay?” David said. “They're assholes,” Donny muttered. David grasped his shoulders to make him move outside, away from them.

He heard Maria cry, “We're here!”

The vaporetto eased toward a pier marked with the name of their stop. David hoisted Donny and hurried to gather their suitcases, leaving Maria to fend for herself. The three young people shook open hands at them and called, “Oh, mama!”

On the pier, luggage at her feet, Maria gazed helplessly and wondered if she could find a room at David's hotel. He shrugged and told her to try.

They moved through a narrow pathway between building fronts and found themselves on a cobblestone street. Maria consulted her map and pointed ahead. In a minute they moved through an open square deserted of people, the wheels of their luggage rattling over the stones.

The Hotel Giorgione was small and neat. Maria peered inside and said its lobby seemed very nice. When

David pulled at the door, it was locked. His watch read past two a.m. He rapped on the glass until a clerk appeared, a bald man with a cardigan sweater under his suit jacket. He unlocked and held the door open a crack. David identified himself, and the clerk shrugged. "We have no rooms, signore."

"I made a reservation. I sent a deposit."

"I remember your name, signore. But your deposit never arrived. We could not hold the room without it."

David wanted to hit the man, slap his thick brown glasses across the lobby.

"Listen! It's the middle of the night. We're exhausted. I gave my travel agent a check six goddamn weeks ago!" Donny sat on the cobblestone and sprawled back against a suitcase. Maria just listened, as if storing away another anecdote.

"I can do nothing, signore." The clerk withdrew and quickly bolted the door, leaving them outside.

David had an urge to stand in the middle of the campo and roar frustration, bellow until he woke up every sleeping soul in Venice.

"I wonder what we'll do," Maria said, looking up at him with her thick face as if the three of them were a unit.

He tried to speak calmly. "Let's just find San Marco. There's got to be something there."

David made Donny drag one suitcase, Maria the other. He lugged her collection of bags, straps over both shoulders, handles in the crooks of his arms, up and down the steps of bridges that seemed to cross and re-cross the same winding canal. With no streetlights, with the moon buried in cloud, the darkness swallowed them. He knew they were lost, wandering randomly in a city of strangers.

They finally saw other people, a couple, two young lovers hand in hand, sitting on church steps. In broken English, on a pocket map under a penlight, the couple traced a route back the way they had come, but when they moved away David couldn't remember any of it.

He decided to follow a single street wherever it led. In front of a small hotel with a polished wooden door a group of drunken men stopped their singing to swarm about Maria, crooning Italian endearments. One dropped to his knees and seized her hand, smacked a kiss on her knuckles. Another stroked her hair. She just stood in the middle of them grinning foolishly. Although his instinct was to abandon her, David pushed through, seized her arm, and pulled her away.

"Arrivederci," the men chanted after them, "Arrivederci," and dissolved into laughter. Donny started laughing too, just as loudly, the first amusement he had shown since David found him staring at a wall in the airport.

Maria dropped the suitcase and ran off, shoes pounding at the stones with heavy steps. At the first side street, no more than an alley, she swerved and disappeared.

Still burdened with her baggage, David seized Donny's shoulders and shook, suddenly furious. "You humiliated her."

"What about those guys?"

"All day she tried to be nice to you."

"She's an ugly pig."

David slapped him, felt the sting radiate up through his arm. The boy stared back, refusing to admit pain. Then David calmed. "You take both carts and follow me."

With Maria's bags bulging at his side, David could barely fit into the alley. He considered dropping them, then wondered if he'd been able to find his way back, if they would still be there.

It was a long passageway, windowless outer walls looming on both sides, warehouses perhaps or factories, built by people who didn't care about light. He turned back to made sure Donny was trudging behind with the carts. Their rumbling seemed muffled now.

He saw a sliver ahead, not really a light, just a shaft of grey glow less dense than the darkness. This is ugly, he kept thinking, bleak and ugly. On an ugly street on an ugly night seeking a ugly women followed by his ugly son.

And now he understood why he had made this trip—to take Donny far from Virginia, fleeing from fear that knowing his son would make her realize she would never find the life she had hoped for in him.

Then he stumbled over something soft, and the heft of the baggage toppled him forward until he sprawled across a tiny square at the end of the alley, a place barely wider than the length of his body. When he pulled himself up, he saw Maria huddled against a brick wall, her arms wrapped around her ankles, her face pressed deep between her knees. He had tripped over her.

In a few seconds he realized the strange yowling noise was her sobbing, a crying unlike any he had ever heard before, a terrible animal misery.

"What's wrong?" he asked, though he was too exhausted to care.

"It's so awful."

"What?"

"Everything." And she fell into an even louder wailing.

David began to reach out, as if there were no choice but to comfort her. But something stepped on his hand. He yelled and looked up at the thin bare leg of the woman from the vaporetto. She was wearing spiked heels. When he tried to pull his hand free, she shifted her weight and the jagged pendant dangled over him.

"Hey? What're you doing?"

She gestured back toward the darkness with her chin, and the others appeared, the round woman, the man in the turtleneck. Something glinted in his hand.

The round woman seized Maria's hair and pulled her head back, arching her neck, shouting something, a single harsh word over and over again. David expected the man to swipe out and slash across her throat, blood to suddenly spurt over them all.

"Do you want money?" he made himself plead. "Credit cards?"

The man reached down and seized David by the back of the head and yanked him upward until they were face to face, grinding his nose into David's cheek. He reeked of a sweet aftershave like an ointment on his skin.

This is death, David thought, and the sensation of an absolute emptiness shuddered through him.

"Bastards! Goddamn fucking bastards!" Donny lunged toward them swinging a suitcase in a wide circle, thumping the man behind the knees, knocking his legs out from under him. The man tumbled atop David, then scrambled off into the alley. The two women backed against a wall, kicking and pointing at Donny, twisting their hands into some obscene gesture.

When the boy stood panting in the square, they screamed convulsively, the man too, next to them now, the three of them shaking their arms in the identical gesture. Then the tall woman did her jerky dance and spit at Maria. The three spun and ran into the darkness, roaring "Oh, mama!" again and again.

Donny tried to hurl the luggage after them. It crashed on the cobblestones, splitting open and spewing clothing. David stared, trying to recognize each item, which of the twisted garments was his and which was his son's. When he turned, Donny was beside Maria, the two of them clasping each other, sobbing and clinging, as if their grief was endless.

Through the space between two buildings, past the tiled roofs, David could make out a narrow view, the glittering edge of a golden dome, a slice of distant sea. And he knew that whatever happened next, he was seeing as much of Venice as would ever matter to him. For months, Virginia had memorized a city from picture books—churches, squares, and palaces. But he had found another Venice, nothing like the one she had dreamed. He felt so sad for her that he wanted to weep.

Then he sensed the swelling of his hand. Something is broken, he thought. David touched the purple flesh with a fingertip and suddenly reeled. He cried out, blinded by the intensity of his pain. Through the tear blur he saw his son reaching up to him as if they were bound by a single hurt.

SUSAN O'NEILL

Brooklyn Summer Rain

Five-thirty in the morning is not Tanya's favorite wakeup. She wriggles her stiff torso into the stiffer leather seat of the couch. A life-long night-owl, she's spent only three hours in bed.

She's alone in her apartment lobby. It's a smallish no-doorman building; who can afford a doorman in Brooklyn these days?

She's here to solve a crime.

> How much of a crime is somebody ripping off your *New York Times*?

That's the thing, though. Steal somebody's car—not that she has one—you piss them off big-time. But...there's insurance, even a new car, maybe—so you score some compensation for your pain.

Steal a woman's *Times*, and there's no redemption for the aggrieved.

Not to mention no Front Page; no Entertainment. No puzzle.

The guys upstairs, Clark and Buddy, went full-on electronic the week after everybody's print *Times* started going MIA. As for the others, Monica and Kevin buy theirs now from Hoagie's bodega, and the other three subscribe to the *Wall Street Journal*. Tonya knows; she's asked around. Everybody else has adapted.

Tanya herself bought the *Times* from the bodega once, but it killed her to do it—not because she begrudged the owner the money; Hoagie's a stand-up guy in a scrappy neighborhood, and she kicks him business when she can—but because it reminded her that some sticky-fingered jerk was putting her to unnecessary hassle and expense.

She gets the electronic version on her computer, a perk of the pricy subscription package. But she wants her *paper* paper. That's what she's paying all that money for. You can't fold an electronic page, park your coffee cup on it, put pen to puzzle—

Yes, *pen*. It gets messy from Thursday on, what with the writeovers, but damn it—she does it in *pen*.

She rubs her eyes. She can see her paper right now, in the no-man's-land entrance between the apartment building's glass doors—the inner door locked, the outer not. It leans against the base of the buzzer-panel wall, the only *Times*, wrapped in blue plastic, dumped there by a delivery person amid three clear-plastic-wrapped *Journals*.

Nobody steals the *Wall Street Journal*.

Rain trickles down the outer door. She scratches her snaggled curls. *I could just open the door and grab the fucking paper, and go back to bed.* Then at least she could do the puzzle before her afternoon shift at the hospital.

You're awake, *idiot. Don't be a wuss.*

Anyway, it's Tuesday. The puzzle's too easy on Tuesday.

She yawns.

She woke this morning—*bing*, awake! She *never* does that. Just sprung up, reliving the call she'd made yesterday to the *Times*. She'd mashed her Galaxy against her ear—probably gave herself brain cancer—nibbling her toast over her paperless table, listening for fifteen minutes as a computer told her how "valuable" the *New York Times* considered her. Then this agent, "Tom," came on and told her, politely, that the company could do squat—how could they know it wasn't somebody, or somebodies, *inside* the building?—to which she argued about finding blue wrappers tossed on the steps. *Outside.* So he gives her yet another "credit" for yet another missed paper...You'd think they'd stop giving her credits after three weeks, right? And maybe take an interest in where the hell their paper was going?

Right.

Rain slaps the outside glass door; early sun backlights the gray beyond.

She stares at the outer door with sandpaper eyes. Wills it to open—

It opens.

He is tall, thin, his face hidden behind the edge of a black umbrella.

She holds her breath.

He stoops and snatches the blue-wrapped *Times*. And disappears with a splash-snap of the outer door.

She springs off the couch, through the two doors, into the rain—bare feet, sweatpants, ripped T-shirt—after him. She hasn't thought this through, what she'll do if she catches him, like that old joke about the dog finally catching a car—but if she's going to be up at five-fucking-thirty-a.m., she is *not* going back to bed without her Times.

He's opening the lobby door of the apartment building on the corner (*ripping off more papers?*) when she catches up. "Hey—hey, you."—wet, breathless with exertion and triumph—*"You!"*

The man turns. One hand clutches the umbrella's curved handle; the other holds several blue-plastic-covered newspapers.

She frowns up into his face.

She expects a teenager, or one of the corner guys, nickel-diming to pay for breakfast or a fix. But his hair is gray; his brown eyes wary. He glances at her, then away.

"Hoagie?" she says, too loud.

He looks at the wet, deserted street beyond them.

She shivers with rain. “I want my *Times,* Hoagie.”

He looks at the papers in his hand as if surprised.

“That’s *my Times.*” She reaches out. “I paid for it.”

He hesitates, then clips the umbrella shaft between arm and chest and lays a paper gently on her palm. He backs up a step. “Sorry—“ He raises his hand,

“No harm, no foul.”

A beat. “Okay.” She turns on a bare heel, clutching her *Times* to her wet T-shirt.

She has her paper.

And will continue to have it, she is certain.

Certain feels hollow.

Certain is his bodega, two blocks away—her coffee-on-the-run, her Snickers bar dinner, the odd carton of eggs when her refrigerator is empty. *Certain* is their banter about politics, the weather, climate change; all this fucking Brooklyn summer rain.

She bought the *Times* there two days ago. *Fuck.* The Sunday *Times.* Briefly noted the fold in it; new delivery configuration, she supposed.

The rain lifts as she reaches the outer glass door to her apartment, but her eyes are damp. She opens it and walks past three untouched *Wall Street Journals* in their clear plastic sleeves. Digs in the pocket of her sweatpants for her inner-door key.

Well. She has her paper.

MIRIAM POLLI

From *Rosina*

When Bartolomeo returns from New York, he is morose, visibly upset by the news that they must hide, or dispose of, any literature in their possession. The New York chapter validated fears of the authorities breaking into suspicious homes. Bartolo, in his nervous habit, pulls and twists his mustache. "If no evidence is found, it doesn't matter. If you're one of the chosen, they'll manage to plant incriminating proof to use against you."

A few days later, the front page of the *Globe* reports that one of the men who was being held in New York turned informer—giving out names of so-called Galleani destructionists, had thrown himself out of an office building window.

"We'll never know the truth. Whether there is a list of names or not," Nicola says, lowering the paper to his lap. Newspapers sprout on the braided rug next to his chair. Dante is kneeling at the coffee table, eye-level with his finger-sized metal cowboys and Indians making war noises.

Nicola reads the headline out loud:

"RED'S DEATH— PLUNGES 18 STORIES."

"Anyone who doesn't agree with their politics is a Communist," he says.

Rosina calls to Dante, "Take your toys in your room, *caro. Andiamo.*"

Preparing for an early start to meet Bartolomeo the next morning, Nicola shaves his beard over the bathroom sink. Rosina already under the thinning cotton blanket in bed, hears him say, “We have to pick up Mario Buda’s car in Bridgewater at the repair shop, and then we’re going to gather as many materials as we can and bring it over to the warehouse so they can be destroyed.”

“We must start to be more careful about what we say in front of Dante,” her voice louder than usual. “He’s getting older now. He’s still young enough to understand or, rather, misunderstand a lot of what we’re saying.”

Nicola sits on the edge of the bed and acknowledges her with a grunt. She’ll have to talk about this further when she has his full attention.

“Do you have to go with Bartolomeo tomorrow?” Rosina asks as he performs his nightly ritual of adjusting the blanket over them. “I really need you here to help me with the packing.”

“I must do this *one* last thing before we leave. Bartolomeo doesn’t know all the stops, all the places as well as I do. Once we get the car, it won’t be long. We’re only going to a few locations to pick up literature and dispose of it. Aldo already has a few teams out.”

There’s no sleep for her now. She’s fired up. Her body tingles, her legs restless. Maybe it is the excitement of their trip. Ah, but now she realizes this familiar sensation; this uneasy lavish, warm feeling that courses through her body. This is the same way she felt when she was pregnant with Dante. An inner glow, lit with a kind of happiness. Smiling to herself, something she’d also been doing a lot of these days. She makes the decision to wait until they arrive in Italy to break the news to Nicola and Dante. A celebration with the whole family.

* * *

Rosina decides to take another suitcase for the small gifts she made and purchased for Nicola's family. She wishes Nicola were home to help her make some decisions on what clothes of his to pack. All morning she's felt a sneaking foreboding—a premonition that something was about to happen. She blames it on her fear of change, even the good kind. Leaving the security of home. Packing. *Such a long passage to Italy. So much could occur.* Since her marriage to Nicola, she relishes the idea of life built around a sense of permanence: Before going to bed each night, as she places her metal wedding band in the tea-rose porcelain cup Nicola found in the Salvation Army, and then slips her misshapen big toe out of her molded slippers, comforted by knowing they'd still be at her bedside each morning. Small rituals—a meditation of their lives, not taken for granted, anchors her to the illusion of a secure existence.

She settles her thoughts by reminding herself she was this way when she carried Dante; this was merely an overall sensitivity to things that didn't seem to matter at any other time. Like the way she broke down and cried when she'd found she overwatered the ivy plant, killing it, then telling Nicola, "I can't even take care of a plant, how can I take care of a baby?" Moments later, the two of them laughed at the absurdity of her words.

She remembers to pack some of Dante's baby clothes for one of Nicola's sisters, but now removes one item from the suitcase. The sailor suit, a romper with a marine-blue trimmed collar, was the first piece of clothing she made for Dante. She was so proud of it. A boy or girl could wear it easily. Fingering the cloth, she again changes her mind. *I can always make another.* She wraps it in brown paper and puts it back in the suitcase, on top of her magenta cardigan.

Rosina falls asleep in Nicola's chair in the parlor. Hours later she wakes from Dante's call. "Mama...Mama." Dante had been having bad dreams at night and, dazed from her own unexpected deep sleep, she hurries to his bedside.

"It's okay, Mama is here." She holds him; wipes the perspiration from his hairline. "You know it's just a dream. Dreams don't come true."

Having heard this before Dante acknowledges by shaking his head pitifully. Rosina is disoriented. Why wasn't Nicola home yet? *He never stayed out this late.*

The ritual of getting Dante back to sleep takes only a few minutes, and once he is sleeping, she tiptoes from his room only to find herself pacing from the kitchen to the parlor.

Maybe they were in an accident. Perhaps the garage didn't repair the car properly, and the vehicle broke down again. They probably got lost, or it's just taken them longer than Nicola thought. She sees no light coming from Mr. Kelley's house. Still, she wants to ask to use his telephone to call Bartolo at his boarding house. Three in the morning. How could she wake everyone up at this unreasonable hour?

Sitting in Nicola's chair once again, she lifts the newspaper from the top of the pile:

PALMER WARNS NATION: NEW
TERRORIST PLOT
TO OVERTHROW GOVERNMENT
WILL ERUPT ON MAY DAY

Sick of seeing the name Palmer, she tosses the paper aside. May Day was well over, and nothing happened. Hopefully, people were catching on to his "fear tactics."

On the dining table, she sees Nicola's keys. Under the keychain are their tickets for passage to Genoa. The name of the ship is printed on the envelope: *Vi da il benevento a bordo Il Dante Alighieri,* and beneath in English, *Dante Alighieri welcomes you.*

Nicola had told her, "Let's not tell our boy the name of the ship. I want to surprise him." Rosina had just finished pressing the pleats in his slacks, put the iron back on its plate. "It won't matter to him, he's too young. It will just be a name to him."

Overwhelmed by the preparations for their trip, she had tossed off the remark, "What's in a name anyway?" And just at that moment, she remembered Ferdinando. She stole a glance at Nicola, reading the *Globe*—and was glad he hadn't been paying attention.

Rosina's neck is sore from the wooden armrest of the settee, uncertain if this is what wakes her, or the heavy banging on the screen door. Alarmed, she suddenly remembers why she is on the sofa. Nicola's keys on the table come to mind, and she rushes to let him in. Through the small glass panel in the door, she sees the frame of a taller man with a long, thin neck. As she gets closer, she recognizes Aldo's pale, narrow face. Fear rises in her chest as she opens the door. Aldo's growing goatee makes him look grubby.

"It was a trap." Aldo touches her elbow, "Come sit down," as he guides her to the settee. "They were arrested. We've already got a group together." Aldo talking at the speed he usually does. "We'll have them out in no time."

Alarmed and confused, Rosina asks, "Who was arrested?" Fear prickles through her. "What happened?"

"Nicola and Bartolomeo were on the streetcar...."

"Arrested? Streetcar? What happened to the car?"

"I don't know for sure, but I think it wasn't ready, or it was part of the trap."

"A trap?"

"They were pulled off the car and arrested as "suspicious characters."

"Suspicious characters?"

She only seems capable of repeating Aldo's words.

"They'll probably be home this afternoon. Our compatriots, *nostri Fratelli* are working on it right now."

She hadn't noticed how really tall and thin Aldo is, but now he seems spare. How can he stand so straight without hunching over?

He rattles off slogans, "defense committee, political arrest, unlawful," words that reach into her like one stitch at a time. Rosina's insides being pulled with each word—darning her tighter and tighter, layer by layer until Aldo's parting statement: "Courage...*Coraggio*, Rosina."

Alone in the parlor, her gut goes taut as if one small, tiny sound from her will rip her open. She puts her clenched fists to her lips, and then, so not to wake Dante, she pushes the needlepoint pillow from the settee over her mouth—to smother her sobs.

Hours later, she moves methodically through Dante's breakfast. Prepares only toast—dresses him and herself to take him to the new nanny, Mrs. Hayes, a friend of Aldo's mother. Aldo had said, "She's sympathetic to our cause, and has agreed to be available whenever needed."

Rosina immediately liked her appearance, a plump, motherly woman, who had her own little boy that Dante could play with. On the walk back from the nanny's, the day holds brilliant sunshine, so bright she notices sharp shadows everywhere. Too much light for such a dreaded day ahead. Last night was only a small nightmare she tells herself. Today it will be over, and tomorrow we will leave for *Italia*. She decides to make pasta with ragu sauce for Nicola for dinner, and tries desperately not to imagine him being jailed overnight.

When she returns to the house, she sees a police car and two mounted police horses tied to the porch column, and her front door wide open. As she steps onto the porch, an officer asks, "Are you Rose Sacco?"

Stunned by his presence, she nods her head.

"Don't move," he says. A halting hand in her face. "Stay there until I tell you it's okay to come in."

From where she stands, she hears drawers or closet doors banging. In the kitchen, the silverware drawer sounds like it's being emptied into the sink. Rosina turns away from the door and sees a grouping of black butterflies on the lilac bush. They rest on a gnarled stem pumping their wings as though unable to fly, yet seconds later, lift off. She remembers the pamphlets under the porch. Nicola's gun in the shoebox on the shelf in their bedroom closet. Her nausea rises.

She doesn't know how much time has passed before the oversized officer allows her to enter the house. At first, she sees her cushions on the settee thrown to the floor—books spread opened, scattered everywhere. The philodendron plant that Nicola had trained to climb is turned over, ripped in half, pulled from the curtain rod. Broken pieces of the clay pot and soil are on the windowsill and floor. An officer comes from the bedroom, swinging an opened suitcase, "You wops planning to go somewhere? Guess you'll have to cancel your trip." When he flings the open luggage, she feels something drop inside her. "Come on, boys, we're done here." Two other cops appear from the back rooms, and as they walk towards the door, she hears them laughing, and one of them says, "Did you see those tits? These I-talian women aren't so bad looking. She could make me happy." More laughter.

Rosina rushes to lock the door after them. She walks through the rooms like a stunned deer she had seen in the field weeks ago. In Dante's bedroom, she sees busted toys, his bed turned over, then unexpectedly, her legs crumble under her, and she plummets to the ground. "*Bastardi*, fucking bastards," she cries out.

Remembering Nicola's pistol, she climbs over the sheets and blankets that are thrown onto the floor in their bedroom. Now at the foot of their bed, she sees the top shelf of the closet, and the box appears to be untouched. Suddenly she knows she will be sick and rushes into the bathroom, where personal items from the medicine chest are strewn about. The heavy oak door of the chest hangs from the loose hinge. Cold sweat tingles through her, stomach clenching, she kneels over the toilet bowl and releases its contents right on top of the bottle of aspirin bobbing in the water. Her washed menstrual cloths also thrown about. She picks one off the floor and wipes her mouth with it.

She can't seem to move. *Susan where are you?* She hears her father's voice: *I knew no good would come from such a man whose ideas are so dangerous to himself and his family.* She covers her ears with the palms of her hands as if to block out his voice. *How? How do you prepare for such a thing?* "Get up," she screams out loud, "you're no good to anyone sitting here. Do something."

In the bedroom, she lifts the sheets, blanket, and pillows and tosses them onto the bed. She takes up what's left of Sinclair's *The Profits of Religion* and places the loose pages back on the night table, then suddenly remembers the boxes of literature under the front porch, and adrenaline in full gear, she races to see if they're still there.

Outside, it already feels like the heat of summer. The earth is warm on her bare knees. The boxes appear untouched. She had never bothered to see them before. It looks like three of four boxes of pamphlets. Nicola's wheelbarrow leans against the side of the house, and when she sees it, she decides to wait until dark to remove them.

Back in the bathroom, she salvages what she can and prepares a hot tub for herself. Aldo will pick her up soon to go to the courthouse. She must try to fix herself to look like the wife of a gentleman. She will spend extra time on her hair. She wants to make a good impression on the judge. He will see that Nicola is not a bad person, just a man with ideals—like the rest of us. If she must, she will stand straight and tall and tell him that Nicola is an ordinary man, just one more sensitive to the human condition, a person who wants to better the lives of the working people, nothing more. She will tell the judge when a mouse comes into their home, she is the one who must find it and kill it. When she prepares the cacciatore, she is the one who must twist the neck of the chicken. The judge will see. *He will understand,* she says out loud, as she presses the light rouge powder Susan had given her onto her cheeks.

From the novel *Rosina* (2025)

RONNA WINEBERG

ARTIFACTS

Nina is sixty-seven and has joined a dating website. There is something odd but exciting about being on her own at this juncture in life—not widowed, but recently divorced—scouring a site to find a match. A companion. As she studies the photos of men online, she feels young and energetic, but when she glances at herself in the mirror, she sees a pleasant face, a once-pretty face, wrinkles fanning the sides of her green eyes, a few wrinkles on her cheeks, snaking down her neck. A respectable face for a woman her age. But no longer young.

She applies makeup before leaving for her date tonight, and uses a magnifying mirror—her vision is not as precise as it once was: white powder on her eyelids as the salesman at Bloomingdale's suggested; she draws a dark shadow on the crease of her lid to create the illusion that her eyes are wide. Then she applies mascara, foundation, blush, lipstick. She slips on her round tortoiseshell eyeglasses, making a mental note to buy a more fashionable pair. She'll go to Warby Parker and find something dramatic, chic.

The strangest thing about aging, she thinks, is that inside she feels more and more like herself, but to the outside world she appears less and less like the younger self still alive inside her.

*

It is six thirty, a cold night in early January, and she sits on the crosstown bus, going to the Upper West Side. Remnants of the holidays—wreaths and strings of lights—still grace some of the buildings the bus drives past.

Rick Friedman lives in an apartment on Riverside Drive, in one of the grand old elegant buildings, he said. She has always loved that part of the city, though in the winter the wind is merciless, and it can be almost impossible to walk there then because of the force of the weather. She lived in a tiny apartment on Riverside Drive decades ago, when her ex-husband was in graduate school, before they moved to Milwaukee and then back to New York.

She's written Rick's address on a piece of paper, to be sure she won't forget it.

He wanted her to see his apartment and invited her over for Italian food. "My favorite," he said.

"Will you cook?" she said.

"Of course not. This is New York. We'll order out, and get it delivered."

This is the first time she has gone to a date's apartment, and she's a little wary. However, she is a grown woman, a grandmother, she tells herself, and has had dinner with Rick three times. Twice on the East Side, once on the West Side, as if he is keeping score, or maybe she is, making sure everything is geographically balanced. He seems smart, decent, appealing even, more so than most of the other men she has met online.

He doesn't seem to have more than the usual accumulation of baggage in his past: two marriages, two divorces, last divorce four years ago. Kids from each marriage who seem to be doing reasonably well as he's related it. He left the first wife for the woman who became his second wife. She eventually left him. Forty years of marriage total. Both wives were in the medical field, like he is, one a doctor, the other a nurse. Rick is a nephrologist.

"I've never dated a teacher," he said.

Nina laughed. "Then maybe you'll learn something." And tonight, she hopes she will, too.

*

Nina is an art teacher and now does substitute teaching. She also volunteers, working one-on-one with middle school students in Harlem, helping with reading skills. Her ex-husband taught economics at a college, and, in a sense, she was more ambitious than he was. She went back to school for a master's in counseling. She has worked as a school counselor, administering tests and counseling parents and children. She's fluent in Spanish, an asset in her work. She suggested her ex-husband consult with businesses and go to conferences. He did this grudgingly. She knew he enjoyed it, though, the recognition, the extra money. He was the kind of man who liked to be in control and didn't like change until he decided to change his life and leave. He moved to New Mexico, remarried, and now lives in the wilderness. He doesn't resurface in Nina's life except on occasion, when he comes to New York to see their grandchild. Sometimes they all meet for brunch at their daughter and son-in-law's apartment—Nina, her ex-husband, their children, their grandchild, her ex-husband's new wife. These gatherings are awkward for Nina but have become a new tradition, the sequela of a late divorce, she thinks. She wants to please their daughter, who likes the family to be together.

There was an unexpected poignancy the last time Nina saw her ex-husband, two months ago. He looked older to her, his brown hair completely gray, his shoulders slumped, a tension in his jaw. He walked over to her at the brunch, standing too close, she thought, telling her that his tennis elbow and right hip had become so painful he was considering surgery. Then he handed her a photograph he'd taken of Zoe, their granddaughter. "Here, sweetie," he said to Nina. "I thought you'd like to have this." He used the same endearing and loving tone he'd used when things were good between them. She took a step back from him. Still, his words made her heart catch.

*

Rick is a nephrologist at a university. In truth, she's not sure about him, just as she's not sure about so many things. She has become less certain as she's grown older. Rick is in his middle or late seventies. She doesn't know his exact age; everyone subtracts years from ages online. She wonders whether something unexpected will happen to him, his health—maybe he's too old for her. Really, she worries about becoming attached to a man again, facing another rupture, a split. To be widowed confers a nobility, she thinks, but divorce is a failure, in her mind. Though an end to a new relationship begun online can't compare to the end of a thirty-year marriage. But perhaps the ending of illusions is what hurts the most.

The last time she and Rick were together, he joked about taking her to a great Greek restaurant in Queens. They could drive in his car there. "Of course," he said, "you don't know if I'm a serial killer." He laughed, and she did, too.

She doubted it, but she'd googled him and found his profile on the university site.

*

The building is an elegant old red brick structure facing Riverside Park. White stone cornices line the top of the building, and white molding surrounds the windows. Nina checks the address twice. She walks into the lobby, which is under construction. There is an abandoned air. Three tall ladders and sheets of new drywall lean against the wall; part of the ceiling is open. The sharp smell of fresh sheet rock fills the space, and for a minute she's a little disoriented and wonders if this is the right place. She spots the doorman behind a desk at the far end.

She walks over to him. "Rick Friedman," she says.

The man nods, picks up the phone, and announces she's here. "Elevator is that way," he says, pointing.

She walks past cans of paint lined up in the hallway, wondering how many other women the doorman has directed to Rick's apartment.

On the tenth floor, she finds his door. She takes a deep breath, slips her eyeglasses into a case in her purse, and pauses, then knocks.

Rick opens the door immediately. "Come in," he says. "You found the place."

"Yes," Nina says. "Nice to see you."

She is tall and fairly slender for her age, with brown shoulder-length hair, her waist thicker than it used to be. Rick is a few inches taller than she is. He's not heavy, but solid, broad, with a bit of a belly from what she can see, well-preserved, with a handsome face, an upturned nose, gray eyes, and almost a full head of thinning gray hair. He looks appealing tonight, she thinks.

He smiles, brushes his lips against hers in a way too familiar for their relationship. "I'll take your coat."

She slips out of her blue down coat, putting her hat in the pocket. He hangs up her coat in the closet. There is something formal about the gesture, awkward, and she wonders if the whole evening will be like this.

She is wearing gray wool pants, a black sweater, boots, a gold necklace with a charm of a heart, and gold earrings. He wears brown corduroy pants, a white shirt, and a black wool vest. Somehow even in the casual clothing, he seems formal.

The apartment has a cavernous feel, and sprawls. There are several hallways, and they walk down one now.

Nina is reserved, but determined to fight against this. She wasn't reserved with her ex, until the end when they had problems and she folded into herself then. One of her resolutions—she believes in making New Year's resolutions—is to be less reserved, to climb out of herself.

Her dinners with Rick haven't been formal, but there is something about being in his home, his space, that brings this out. She looks around, and her thoughts are clicking. The ceilings are high, with molding, and the apartment has been renovated, has a modern spacious feel, an elegance. Japanese prints of landscapes hang on the walls, and prints of flowers, carefully placed and aligned. She is surprised. This is more of a home than she expected.

"You have lovely things," she says.

"Thanks." He smiles with pride. "I'll give you a tour, if you'd like."

They walk into the living room. The windows look out onto the Hudson River. The lights of New Jersey twinkle in the distance.

"This couch," he says with disdain, "was from my marriage. My ex-wife wouldn't let me take the couch that would fit here. I'm going to get rid of this."

She nods. It's a gray corduroy couch with huge pillows, a little worn, too big for the space, and sits in front of the windows. "You'll find something else."

"I'm still organizing. I still have stuff in boxes."

The white cabinets and counters in the kitchen are gleaming. Nothing looks out of place. The counters are mostly bare. She wonders if he even eats here.

"This way." He escorts her down another hallway. At the end is a room he describes as a den, with a couch, television, and bookshelves. "My kids sleep here when they're in town. The two who live in Denver. I wanted a lot of space. A nice place. My wife was the one who left. I told you. She wanted to keep every last thing we owned, didn't want to give an inch. She told me, 'I'd like an open marriage.' I said, 'Fuck you.'"

"Sounds like she was angry. You were angry. I know about anger in a marriage, from my own."

"God knows what the problem was. She's not happy now. My therapist says possessions mean nothing. Let everything go. Move on. That's what I'm doing."

Nina nods again.

Rick's jaw tenses for a minute, then relaxes.

He has told her about his therapist. She's told him she is seeing one, too. What you don't say, she thinks, is that a whole industry has developed around divorce, professionals whose purpose is to guide people through divorce and the aftermath—the lawyers, analysts, accountants, psychologists who treat one or both partners and sometimes the children. An endless list, and Nina is relieved this is mostly behind her.

Rick pulls a book off a shelf. "This prayer book belonged to my grandmother. There's writing in the back. Hebrew. You're a nice Jewish girl. Can you read it?"

She laughs. She isn't sure if his calling her a girl is flattering or condescending or a joke, a figure of speech. "No one has called me a girl for a long time. Or nice, in the same sentence." She flips through the pages. "I can't read much. A few words. Here. *Shalom. Mayim.* Water."

"Someday I'll have it translated. No one is all that nice anyway, I've come to believe."

They walk back into the hallway, and he stops at a closed door. "This is why I'm here, in this apartment." He pulls open the door. Behind it is a large walk-in closet, almost the size of a small room. Shelves line the walls, floor to ceiling, filled with sculptures, vases, wooden and ceramic bowls, jugs, pitchers, clay pots, figures of people. "I'm interested in South American and Mexican art, Egyptian, old artifacts. It's my retirement."

"This is like a museum." Nina eyes the collection. That's what it is, a hidden collection. The objects gleam beneath the fluorescent lights that hang on the closet ceiling. Some objects are painted bright colors, reds, browns, and green pigments, some pink and white, others the color of pale clay, all lined neatly on shelf after shelf. This seems like a portal into another world, another part of Rick.

"Those," he says, "are anthropomorphic. People. And that one..."

"Cycladic art."

"Exactly. Marble. You can only afford small pieces like this. A kandila, a vessel, 3000 to 2800 BC."

She admires the graceful shape, the yellow-white color of the marble. "This one is especially beautiful."

The piece next to the kandila is a foot high or so, a clay sculpture of a house, painted in browns, pinks, and white, the two front doors flung open.

"I thought you'd like to see this. You appreciate art. That one, the house, is from Brazil. Look inside. There are two people. A man and a woman. They're..." He pauses. "Copulating."

She doesn't turn to face him. She looks closely at the figures inside the house. They are fucking, she thinks.

"On the top shelf is something tamer. The jug. Egyptian."

"Where did you get all of this?" she asks.

"Oh, over the years, I've collected it. I found bargains. My ex-wife and I bought some together. I've traveled there—South America, Mexico, Greece, once to Egypt. I gave her the couch. I gave her the apartment. I gave her what she wanted. But I wanted this."

"I can see why."

"I've bought some myself. When I travel, it's for work, to go to a conference or give a talk, but still I've bought things if I could afford it."

On the bottom shelf sits a pile of what looks like Japanese wood block prints, similar to some that hang on the living room walls. "Those?" she asks, turning to look at him. "Will you frame them?"

"Ukiyo-e. From Japan. I don't need to display them. I know they're here. I can appreciate them whenever I want." He steps into the hall. She does, too. He shuts the door.

*

They sit side by side on a couch in the room next to the kitchen, studying the takeout menu from Gargatto's. She thinks about the closet of artifacts. Copulating. An odd word for him to use. Perhaps she and Rick don't know each other well enough for him to state the obvious. But why not? It is a polite word, reserved; perhaps he's picked up on her reserve, restraint. Or maybe that is just who he is.

Her parents never used the word "fucking." When they talked about sex, the few times they did, they said "relations." Did Rick's parents refer to it as "copulating?" Maybe the way she and Rick each speak is part of a generation gap.

She glances up from the menu and realizes there are no photographs here, and the order, the neatness, appeals to Nina. Though his apartment seems like a home, there is a pristine feeling to the rooms, as if they aren't quite lived in, as if Rick hasn't found his place here yet; he has plunged into a new life, ready or not.

Maybe she's projecting. Her apartment, the one she and her ex-husband once shared, still has objects everywhere: from the children's childhoods, drawings they did, books, photographs—even of her ex—books he didn't take with him, her own paints and brushes that sit on the kitchen table. She's thought this makes her apartment seem warm, lived-in. Why has she been keeping all of it? She doesn't need those things to remind her she has a past.

"I've been divorced four years, like you. I lived in a small rental, a studio, for a few years," Rick says. "Stored my stuff and then found this. I wanted a place I could call home. How about penne al vodka?" He points to the menu. "Let's get a few dishes and we can share."

*

He orders dinner, and they talk more about his collection of artifacts. When the food arrives, Nina finds the forks, knives, plates, and napkins in the kitchen. She sets the table in the living room, and she and Rick sit facing one another.

"I'll retire in a few years," he says as they eat. "The university doesn't have a mandatory retirement age. But I'd like to do something else, work with kids, in a school."

"When you're ready," she says, "I can help you get started."

"That's great. I appreciate it. To be honest, I'm a little worried about retiring, though. I'm not in private practice. The 401(k)."

"Your collection, your artifacts. That's your retirement, you said."

"Part of it. I'd hate to sell anything. But I'm not there yet. Who knows what it's really worth? I had to split retirement with my ex-wife. You must have done that with your ex-husband."

"Yes. I'm still working. I figure I'll have what I have when I retire. I try to be careful."

"Of course," he says kindly.

They talk about their children and he asks about her work.

After dinner, she collects their plates and closes the plastic containers that house the ravioli, penne, and salmon they haven't finished. "I can put these in the refrigerator," she says.

"No, I'll get rid of them." He jams the containers into a plastic garbage bag. "Be right back."

Nina watches him warily. He will throw out perfectly good food, waste it, and not recycle the plastic either. "You're going to throw that out?"

"Yes."

"Why don't you save it? It's food. It could be lunch tomorrow. Dinner."

"Well." He considers this. "I'll try that. If you'll come for lunch."

She laughs.

"Okay. I'll save it. Do you want some tea? Coffee?"

"How about wine?"

"Good idea. I don't have much." He swings open the refrigerator door.

She peeks inside. A bottle of Manischewitz Concord Grape sits on the second shelf.

"That's all I have." He sets the containers of Italian food on the shelf, too.

"That's fine," she says. The apartment is put together, she thinks, but the refrigerator is almost empty, except for the wine, an orange, half a gallon of milk, and now the leftovers from dinner, as if the veneer of order, mastery, is here, but something is missing inside Rick.

"What did you present at the conference?" she asks. "You said you've been out of town."

"It's not that interesting."

"To me it is."

He shrugs. "People want answers. I have no answers."

"None?"

"Oh, I can help with certain things. When I was young, younger, I thought I could solve everyone's issues. I was good at diagnosis. I would keep lives going. I'd make great discoveries. I don't have those illusions now. Sometimes I can; sometimes I can't."

"What about your research?"

"Fifteen people used to work in my lab. Now there are two." He shakes his head. "There isn't much money for research grants anymore. Hypertension treatments for cardiovascular disease in patients with chronic kidney disease. I talk about it all day."

He sounds disappointed, Nina thinks. The shrinkage of his lab must be hard for him.

"And your art?" he says.

"I love it. Watercolors and some sculpture. But I'm still teaching, and I work with kids on reading. I have my granddaughter. It's a full life."

"Better not to have too much time on your hands. I'd like to see the watercolors."

They are standing close to each other, so close, and he sets the bottle of wine on the counter, kisses her, and she responds. It is a tentative kiss, his lips fuller than her ex's or the few other dates she's kissed.

Then he steps back, pours wine into two glasses, and he and Nina sit on the couch in the living room. She had forgotten the sweetness of Manischewitz, almost like dessert.

He presses his head back on the pillow of the couch, gulping his wine. "It's *basheret* that we've met," he says suddenly.

"Excuse me?"

"You know. *Basheret*. Meant to be. That we met."

"I didn't know you were religious."

"I'm not. Spiritual. Maybe this wine brings it out." He pours more into their glasses. "I really like you."

She smiles. "I like you."

"Well." He scoots closer. He leans and kisses her again. She likes the feel of his lips on hers and his arm around her. It may not be love—and how could it be, when they hardly know one another—but it feels like enough now, enough of something without a name.

"Manischewitz," he laughs. "An aphrodisiac. Who knew? Part of the seduction."

"A multi-use wine."

"I thought I'd make my move. I'd like... I'd like us to become lovers," he says softly. "Do you want to?"

She sees his neck from an angle she hasn't before. The skin is sagging beneath his chin. And his face. There is something a little wounded about him, his expression. We're all wounded, she thinks, but that vulnerability makes him appealing.

*

His bedroom is next to the living room. He turns on a lamp. Stacks of books and magazines sit on the night tables, an open suitcase on the dresser.

"I haven't unpacked yet from my last trip," he says.

She has entered another country, a space of intimacy, crossed a border. She pulls off her boots, sweater, pants, and he's shedding his clothing, folding it neatly and setting it in the suitcase, as if he is ready to leave on another trip. She looks around the room. There isn't a place for her to put her clothing, so she lays it on top of a pile of magazines, on the journal, *The Lancet*.

She turns around and sees that he is in bed, waiting. A condom sits on the night table next to him now. She takes off her necklace, her earrings, puts them in her pants pocket. The room feels cold, and she's eager for the warmth of his body. She thinks for a moment: what am I doing? And then she doesn't think. She presses her hands against her breasts, hiding them, but then drops her hands to her sides, hurries to the bed, slides next to him.

"Finally," he whispers, "a real kiss."

"Yes," she murmurs.

This is what she has missed, this pleasure. She remembers a student she counseled a few years ago who talked about hookups. The girl liked to hook up with a friend, and called him a fuck buddy. Nina talked to her about commitment and dignity, and thought then: that's the generation gap. But maybe she's wrong. There is no gap. Maybe that's what Rick will become.

She glides her hand down his chest, to his belly, which has extra mounds, mounds of dough, she thinks, but this is what she has to offer, too, an aging, no-longer-firm body that wiggles like Jell-O. His arms have some muscles; he must work out. She moves a hand to his legs; his penis is long and firm—impervious to the insults of age. He kisses her shoulder, her waist, and their bodies entangle. Her breath is quickening and she wonders if she will come, as if she has a choice, but there is a choice—if she will allow herself to be this free with this man. Then he lies on top of her, slides into her, and it is over before it really starts. He comes with a wild groan.

"God, I'm sorry it was so quick," he mumbles, and shuts his eyes. "Damn. I really am."

He is heavy on her, heavier than she imagined he would be. "Rick." She jostles him, and he climbs off her.

"That was so good, Nina. I'm sorry about the speed. It won't be like that next time. How was it for you?"

"It was really nice," she says diplomatically, and it was, though she's a little disappointed. She leans her head on his shoulder.

And then he smiles, kisses her forehead, pulls the quilt over himself, and falls asleep.

She remembers her marriage, when things were rocky, the end in sight. If her husband hadn't left, she would have left him. Nights when they made love wordlessly, and he fell asleep just as they finished, and she lay in bed beside him, but felt utterly alone. It was an odd juxtaposition, maybe not so unusual, she thinks. How many people can you be intimate with? How many people can really assuage a sense of loneliness? Even if that person is your spouse.

She feels this now in Rick's room, in his bed, an essential aloneness, and it is not an unpleasant feeling. She is content, a free agent. She knows she will never again have what people who've been together for a long time, for decades, have. That continuity. The comfort. Or entrenched dissension. She is still getting used to this. But she can have companionship. Is that the most she can hope for? If she's lucky, maybe new love.

Sounds of occasional traffic from Riverside Drive push into the room. The shriek of a siren. The winter wind is whipping against the window, seeping into the room, too. Nina lies on her back beneath the sheet for a long time and then realizes the window is open wide. Rick sleeps with the windows open. She likes the windows closed. She didn't notice before, and she feels chilled.

The white down quilt is wrapped around Rick, and he's clutching the fabric. It would be impolite to wake him, she thinks, or to yank the quilt so she can cover herself, too. There is always something to negotiate in a relationship, even at the beginning, even now. If they knew each other longer, for months, she would wake him.

She moves closer to him and tries to soak in the warmth from his body, from the quilt. After a while, she realizes she won't be able to sleep. She envies him, his ability to tumble into sleep, an intensity as he sleeps. She gets out of bed. If she doesn't sleep, she will be useless the next day.

Faint light floats in from the window, and she gathers her clothing and boots, tiptoes to the living room, and finds her purse on the couch. She traipses to the bathroom in the hallway, next to the closet of artifacts, using the flashlight on her cell phone to guide the way. A navy blue towel hangs on a chrome bar there, folded neatly. She lifts it from the bar, holds part of the towel under the faucet, then quickly washes herself, washes him off her, breaking the code of order here. Then she dries herself with another corner of the towel and gets dressed.

She rinses the corners of the towel and hangs it back on the bar. The towel should dry by the morning; she wants to preserve the order of his apartment. She turns around, catching a glimpse of herself in the mirror. Mascara is smeared beneath her eyes, and her face has a flushed softness to it. She takes a piece of toilet paper, dabs away the rogue mascara.

She finds paper and a pen in her purse, and writes a note:

Dear Rick,

Couldn't sleep. It was really nice. Have to see my daughter early tomorrow. Thank you for tonight, everything. We'll be in touch.

—Nina

She leaves the note on the dining room table. She hopes he will understand. She glances down his hallway again at the closet of artifacts, thinking about the unexpected beauty of the objects hidden there. Then she grabs her coat and shuts the front door behind her. She has never left a date like this. She has never been in this position before. She has to babysit her granddaughter in the morning. But that's an excuse. It is easier, she thinks, to slip away now, into the night, and be in her bed in her own home rather than lie awake and wonder what she is doing here. Here, meaning not just his bed and his apartment, but here, in her life.

*

She makes her way past the rows of paint and the ladders, the sheets of drywall leaning against the walls of the lobby. The doorman's head droops onto his chest, and he's snoring.

Some experiences make her feel fully alive, she thinks. When she and her ex were still in love. Walking outside in the cold or in a snowstorm. Painting. Talking to her daughter or son. Holding her granddaughter. Maybe lying in bed, next to Rick.

Riverside Drive is dark and silent, except for the wind blowing fiercely, pushing so hard against her, as if it is trying to push her back to his building, to his apartment. Her down coat feels as thin as paper. She searches her pockets for her hat. It must have dropped somewhere, maybe in Rick's apartment. She pulls up the collar of her coat. She isn't going to retrace her steps to look for the hat now. She will get it another time. Or not. There will be another time, she hopes. But she can't stay tonight. It feels too intimate, waking up next to each other—if she finally fell asleep—or lying awake all night next to him, still almost strangers. Maybe in time, if things develop. She will see. And so will he.

She thinks about something she once read by Isaac Bashevis Singer. She doesn't remember the exact words: there's always a kinship between souls; souls are either close to one another or far from each other. How do you gauge that kinship? she wonders. She had hopes for Rick. She doesn't know if he and she are that close, their souls. How long will it take to find out?

She soldiers on, turning on Seventy-Eighth Street, and at West End, she sees a taxi in the distance and flags it.

She's been left by men and she's left them, gone on dates; things have fizzled and there has been no resolution, no contact, as if one or the other has fallen off the earth, disappeared. Ghosted. She will call Rick in the morning.

The taxi driver interrupts her thoughts. He's a middle-aged man, balding. "It's late," he says, eyeing her in the rearview mirror, "for you to be wandering around in this cold, a person your age. No offense intended. Good for you. Where are you going?"

"It's a good question," she says, giving him her address. "New York. The city that never sleeps."

"Well, happy New Year. I guess you can still say it, even though the year changed a few days ago. There's no rule. You know, I've made my resolutions. Life is so short. But if you ask me, money is nothing. I work to pay the bills. No more, no less. See everything you can. Do whatever good you can do, whatever it is. That's how I want to live my life."

"That's what I'm doing," Nina says. "Trying to do."

Or is she? She understands the psychology of children, of adults, but after all this time, even though she feels more like herself, she still doesn't quite understand every aspect of herself. She almost asks the man to turn around and drop her at Rick's apartment.

Her heart is hammering in her chest. She realizes she's woozy from the wine. Manischewitz goes down so easily, like water, more potent than she remembered. The only way to see what happens in the labyrinth of a relationship, she thinks, is to move through it. She will step into the labyrinth with Rick, if he's willing.

She leans her head against the seat. She and the driver sit in silence. The man maneuvers the taxi on the transverse through Central Park, and she stares out the front window, straight ahead.

From the collection
***Artifacts and Other Stories* (2022)**

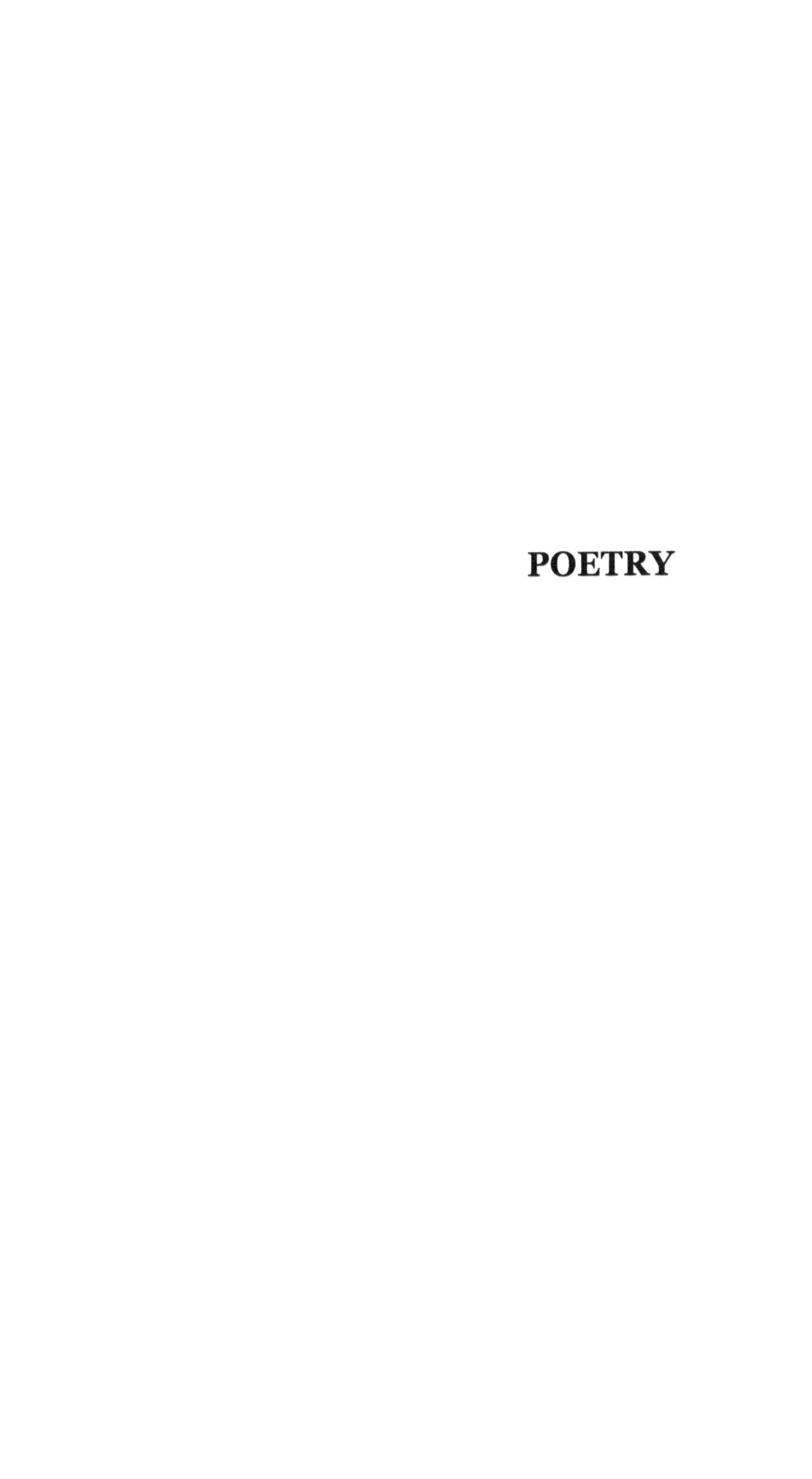

POETRY

CLAIRE BATEMAN

V from *Locals*

In this realm, the population is still reeling from the flash bulletin wedged between a commercial for composting mulch and a public service reminder about the annual anti-aging vaccine.

"Where were you when you heard?"

"I was in a sports bar watching the game—we just put down our drinks, and sat there, staring."

"We were at the mall, shopping in electronics, and all of a sudden, we saw it lit up on a hundred different screens at once"—

floating in blackness, THE WORLD, one moment assumedly planar, the next, indisputably round.

Now everyone's relationship to the horizon has been irrevocably altered, along with their understandings of gravity, heaven and hell, somnambulism, flight, transcendence, and periphery.

Now there is no way off! Gone the possibility of a balletic leap from the edge!—in its place (of all things) only digging, only "down" and "in"—and where's the allure in that?

*

VI from *Locals*

Each morning in this realm, the people check to see that once again during sleep, they have been reincarnated, or more accurately, reinstated, as themselves, complete with personal histories, memory gaps, and ingrown toenails. Themselves, not "still" but "again." Old people: themselves! Pregnant women: themselves! Even the infants and the unborn, though they don't realize it: themselves!

Occasionally, someone stays up all night—though this person may feign normalcy, the excruciating courtesy that friends and family exude only intensifies the shame of being yesterday's version.

*

From the prose poetry collection *Locals* (2012)

BARBARA FROMAN

Petal Shock

You loathe me.

I can tell by the way
you drive dulled prongs
into the soil
and twist.

Or plunge your rusted wedge
into my heart of secrets,
to loose my grip
on life.

I see the way you look at me
when I resist,
the bile rising in
your eyes.

What is it that offends?

Your vapors leave me
breathless, stinging,
withering
on Why?

Don't you know your war is folly?

For even as I wilt,
my sister sheds her crown of
fresh seed tears
to spite your pride.

MARIA MAZZIOTTI GILLAN

Watching the Pelican Die

On TV, I watch the pelican with its mouth wide open,
its wings and body coated with oil. Is it screaming?
I do not hear the sound and since this is a photograph,
I don't know if it was caught in that mouth-stretched howl
when it died or if it's howling
in recognition that it cannot survive the thick coat
of oil that bears it down.

The ladies who take care of you while I'm away tell me
you are having trouble. "His hands," they say, "his hands."
When I come home, I see that your hands have turned black
at the tips and I see that the ends of your fingers
have been eaten away. I watch the dead bird in the Gulf
floating on top of the water, its legs stiff and straight in the
air, its body drained of all motion, all light.

The next day I take you to the doctor; he tells us he will have
to operate to remove the gangrenous flesh.

The announcer on CNN says BP didn't want the photographer
to take pictures of the dying birds
covered as they are with the black slick of oil.
"They were hoping," he says, "that the birds would sink and
the evidence would be swallowed by the ocean."

In the late afternoon, I hear my daughter cry out.
I rush to see what has happened, and you are stretched out on
the bed, your body so thin you look like a boy.
You do not move. I call 911 and the ambulance takes you
to the hospital.

BP is trying to put a cap on the spewing oil rig; the CEO
keeps saying, it's no problem. Clumps of oil wash ashore

and float on the surface of the water. The beach is littered with dead fish and birds.

At the hospital, they want to know whether we want extraordinary measures. "No," I say. "He has a living will." We hover around while they admit you. You have forgotten how to speak. Mostly you lie in bed, staring into a space above our heads.

In my mind I see that screaming bird, its mouth wide open, a picture of torment and despair.

I reach out to hold your hand, stroke your forehead. "Dennis," I call out, "Dennis." You do not hear me.
The doctor comes in to see you. "Well," he says, "he should have been dead five years ago. What did you expect?
You shouldn't have taken such good care of him."

"We did everything we could," the BP president says, looking directly at the camera. "It's not such a calamity," says the governor of Louisiana. "We don't need to stop deep-water drilling. Our economy will collapse if we do."
We stand around your hospital bed. My brother comes in and says he'll try a stronger antibiotic. "It's bad," he says, but he waits until we are in the hall to tell me.

The social worker says, "You should put him in a nursing home." My brother says, "You kept him home all this time. If he gets a little stronger, I'll let him go home and he'll be around the things he knows.

The doctor comes in and says, "He's not going to make it." The social worker admonishes us with her bag of common sense. She does not love you. We take you home.
I sit next to you and hold your hand.

The MSNBC reporter stands on the beach in a hurricane and picks up a huge glob of oil with a stick. "Look," she says, "look," and drips the oil on the white sand. She is shaking with fury at such destruction. Dead birds float behind her.

"I'm in so much pain," you say, though you have not
complained before. Althea feeds you a jar of baby applesauce.
You open your mouth and accept the food. When I see the
pelican on TV with its mouth wide open in horror,
I remember you as you lay dying. On the Gulf, the earth and
the sea are being destroyed, just as you were by the disease
that finally defeated you after you struggled against it for all
those years.

Some things are bigger than all of us. We cannot defeat
them. If there is enough carelessness and greed in the world
even the ocean can be destroyed, and you, who fought
against this illness with such courage, even you
cannot survive, the blackened tips of your fingers, the oil
on the birds feathers, the birds dead and floating on
the surface that gradually sink and disappear.

From *The Silence in the Empty House*

DIANA SENECHAL

Listening

Today I tried something new
(Or old in a new way):
Saying nothing.

True, many stints of null
Had marked my days before,
But this nothing had

A pluck to it.
Tuning, muting
Its strings, gearing

Up for the miracle
(As anything that comes
From zero is miracle),

It befriended the oval.
Later I thought of how
The hush had given me time

To hear space sing,
To see the clouds converge,
Break up, glitter, and

Spatter the long sands,
Daring me into a brief
Collapse of words.

The words resurged,
But with the glint of return
From a private voyage:

"Later I looked up the name
Of that beach whose waves
Rough-sang the sky."

From the collection *Solo Concert* (2025)

RITA SIGNORELLI-PAPPAS

The Chameleon

It's easy to forget her
with the nerve endings
of a rainbow and glands
like elegant rosettes

especially if the blue
door of darkness opens
and catastrophe just stands there
snapping a salute

but then I remember
Hamlet grinning and eating
from her dish as if
he could finally feel

the bright oils of her goodness
rinsing his bones like
a soft stream—and I remember
her green lungs filling with euphoria,

her long tongue leaping
the length of her body
like a ribbon of brocade
to snag a day-flying moth.

Then her quick toes begin to curl
and I remember to grip life's pain
like a branch flung over
an abyss—I remember

the excited lunge of imagination—
my own wild hunger
rushing to seize
winged promises in the air.

From the collection *The Chameleon* (2025)

J.R. SOLONCHE

Barren Road

I have a friend who lives
on Barren Road. It's a
shame he's not a poet.
"It's a shame you're not
a poet," I said. "Why's
that?" he said. "Because
you live on Barren Road,"
I said. "So that's why it's
a shame I'm not a poet?"
he said. "Yeah. Consider
the irony," I said. "I do.
I've been considering it
all the time since it really
was barren," he said. "I'm
surprised at you. This is
the first time you said it's
a shame I'm not a poet.
Well, I think it's a shame
you are. A damn shame.
What a waste of a mind,"
he said. I understand.
He's a sociologist.

Memorial Service for a Potter

Your spirit was there with us, he said.
And I agree that your spirit was there with us
as the spirit of the departed is always there with them.
But where exactly was that I wondered.
Was your spirit in the bumblebee bumping around the tent?
Was your spirit in the woodpecker hammering overhead?
Was your spirit in the river below us
beyond the railroad tracks?
Was your spirit in the big black beetle
crawling on his shoulder
while he was bragging that he was chosen
because he was the only one
who could do it without weeping?
Tell the truth.
Wasn't your spirit in the ceramic cup you made,
the one that leaked white wine on his lap
because he bragged he could do it without weeping?

Both from the forthcoming collection
***Barren Road* (2025)**

EXCERPTS FROM AN INTERVIEW WITH WALTER CUMMINS, by Bill Lawrence

Bill: I'd like to welcome my special guest today. Walter Cummins.

Walter: Glad to be here. Glad to talk with you.

Bill: Let's get into your long career. Lots of exciting publications, a long career of not only writing, but also editing. We'll also dig into the history of Serving House Books. You were the cofounder of this press.

And so we'll get to that. But let's start with you. Let's start with your career as a writer.

Where did that all begin?

Walter: Well, I mean I took a course in college in my junior year, and I was afraid.

I was nervous about taking a creative writing course. I was Writing for the university paper, but not fiction, which is what I ended up doing...

After my 6 months in the National Guard, I was working as a technical editor in New York and editing more than writing. And I had taken a New School course, and I applied to Iowa, and I don't know how I got in. Took me years to get the sense of whatever I was really doing and to start publishing. I tried writing novels. I did get a couple of published, paperback originals, but I am ashamed of them. I haven't read them in decades,

Bill: I read that you didn't write novels.

Walter: Well, I since I gave it up. I wrote some. I'm not a novelist, and I have theories about the kind of interest that a writer has to have and how writers who write novels are really interested in exploring characters.

You know, I have friends who are novelists who want to write short stories, but every time they get an idea they can't control it. And they want to have a character in a short story who's memorable.

But the situation is time. Whereas in a novel, your protagonist, or your multiple characters go through a number of different issues.

But the short story is a one-time thing. So I was much more comfortable doing that.

And I didn't start publishing stories until the early seventies. And then it then it took off. I was a much better storywriter, at least as far as editors were concerned, as far as I'm concerned.

And I stayed at Iowa for five years, because once I got the MFA, I didn't like the job offers I had, so I said, Well, I'll just get a Phd.

And then I was an instructor. It paid me $5,000 a year, so I could afford rent and diapers and things of that sort, but that's when I turned to stories. I was turning them up.

Bill: Were there lots of rejections through the years, too?

Walter: Oh, yes, of course. I guess we all go through it. You know for your first you're saying if I can ever publish one sort story in my life, I will be a happy person, and all the rejections keep coming in. And I mean they deservedly were rejected.

Having been become an editor, I could see why editors would have turned me down. And that's true for everybody. When I was an editor, we were turning down people who had substantial publication records. It just didn't match the style of the press or the journal, or we just didn't think it was for us. Sometimes we just did a story on a subject similar to it an issue ago. And even though this one's okay, we don't want to repeat ourselves, and that sort of thing. And sometimes as editors, sometimes we would publish a story that had been rejected by other magazines, and then also we find stories we rejected. But that's what you're dealing with, you know, subjective judgment. There's no way of measuring any kind of objective way. And young new writers don't always understand that.

Bill: it's not a personal rejection of you as a human being. Or always necessarily skill, right.

Walter: It's the art, and it's time and place, theme, and also the taste. You know, different editors have different tastes. Judgments are made. What I listen to in music, or what I would watch on TV video is a matter of taste.

Bill: Well, at what point did you get into editing?

Walter: I became the Editor of *The Literary Review*. It was a question of who. Who on the faculty can edit?

Bill: So in all those years at *The Literary Review*, did you have readers that screened things before they got to you.

Walter: Once we started an MFA program we had the MFA students who are interested in doing that, of course, and they would screen things and also every once in a while I'd look back and say did they miss something I would have liked? But here you're dealing with hundreds and hundreds of Submissions.

Bill: Wow! That many.

Walter: And then it becomes time. I've rejected 20 pieces today, am I? Am I that nasty a person? And then, there's a just a lot to read. As a writer you feel sympathy for the writer.

Bill: I would be highly suspicious of the editor who's not writing.

Walter: Yeah, how do you get into the field? Right?

I did it all, as I said, for a total of about 20 years.

Bill: So how did you get into the founding of Serving House Books?

Walter: As a magazine editor, I would do a collection by this person or a book by this person. If it's a story writer who had a novel I knew, well, how am I going do this?

Become a book publisher, and then the coincidence was publication on demand, which was in the early two-thousands. And by chance I got involved in working with people who were doing something with publishing.

But colleague and friend, he was just an excellent writer, and he gave me all of his writings, and I did a blog. And then people said "Oh, we'd like to make a book out of this. At the University, I was involved with the people doing the book, because I know nothing about the computer technology. And then I felt comfortable because with the publication on demand, you didn't have to spend a lot of money with a print run, and having a garage full of books, and the postage that's involved.

And at that time, I was teaching in our MFA Program with Thomas E. Kennedy, who had been a friend. Tom and I had done a number of projects together.

We also knew writers, friends who had been with major trade publishers and couldn't get their books accepted again, not because of the literary quality, but because of marketing. They hadn't sold enough and therefore the marketing people are making decisions, and in many cases more than the editorial people. And so we knew a number of people with good books, and we said, let's give them an outlet.

And so then along the way, people obviously heard about the press, and we discovered some other writers and new people who were unknown to us.

So I'm proud of our writers, and the fact that that we were the ones who recognized their ability.

I don't have an accurate count. I think it's about 120 that we did.

Bill: I think it's 125.

Walter: Okay. Well, you did.

Bill: If I counted right.

Walter: And the awards they got. Finalists and shortlisted for awards, and good reviews. When I've gotten to the age where I am, I just couldn't continue, and I didn't see myself as the future, and that's why we, I and others who are in the press, are so happy to have you as the publisher now and with your enthusiasm and ideas, and clear vision of the future.

I do think it's been an important press. And I know that small presses have a short life. It depends on people's sort of attention span, and how much they're willing to put the time to put in.

Tom and I were at that point. But I was still teaching, but I had more time. One of the things we were not interested in was making money. But yeah, we do want to break even. We didn't want to lose money, but we didn't want to make money.

Bill: It wasn't the goal.

Walter: It wasn't. But you know, with print on demand, you can get by, and you can get recognition, and the books can get out there. And our main goal was getting books out into the world. And with the printing change, that was a game changer.

Bill: Did you ever do any small run prints?

Walter: We did with one author who was interested in doing it. He wanted French flaps. I knew what they were, but I never knew the name. And I said, okay, well, I'll look for a printer. So I think in Michigan. But the problem was when you've sold the books. 1,000. I think he had. And you need another 100 books or so. You just want to have some more, it's very difficult to do with printers.

Bill: Yeah, it's very expensive.

Walter: Yes. You know you can get with POD one book, or a hundred books, or 500 books, and it lives forever. The printing quality was probably inferior, but I find that it's hard to tell the difference now.

Bill: That's true. It's really caught up.

Walter: My last book, in terms of producing is for my friend Mark Hillringhouse, and we're at the end. Mark was a friend of the New York poets in the 80s. And he interviewed them. I think about 15 of them. John Ashbury, Kenneth Koch, James Schuyler, Gerry Stern. And those interviews were published, most of them in magazines back then. He has a couple new ones. So we're coming to the end of that. But I think to me it's an important book because of the history of poetry. And these people have become important poets. And what they have to say, and about that world you know, the St. Mark's poetry readings, and the people who are running that, and the rivalries and the jealousies and Mark is also a very good photographer.

I didn't realize that's how he started his career after college. He was hired by the publishers to do all their photographs.

Bill: Wow!

Walter: And then he became a poet himself by hanging out with the New York poets. And but he has a story, the way Tom (Kennedy) and I, started Serving House.

Mark was walking in the East village with a couple of poet writer, friends, and they were standing on the street corner, and they said, let's start a book review, the *American Book Review*. They just started it like that, that casually.

Bill: How, when, and where did you meet Tom (Kennedy)? At what point?

Walter: Well oh, Tom!

Tom submitted a story to *The Literary Review* in the late 80s, and we were just knocked out by the story. This was some writer we didn't know anything about. And then we gave it the award. And he and I got in touch. Tom lived in Copenhagen, but he would come here because he had friends and family.

We got together and started these projects and became friends. And I visited him a few times in Copenhagen.

After his death, we did a book on him that I had started before. Pieces he had written. Excerpts from his various work. I can't remember how many people, about 25 friends who wrote about him. We even had a couple in Danish, that we did. He was a good translator of Danish poetry. Then we did his bibliography. Carefully compiled.

Bill: There's a lot here. It's a great tribute.

Walter: And then Tom, we just had a lot of fun together coming up with ideas. After we formed Serving House Books, we did a couple of books. We did some issues for *The Literary Review* that were also collaborative collections.

Bill: Well, we're forever indebted to you and Tom, and we'll carry on the tradition. I thank you for joining me today to talk.

Walter: Thank you very much for having me. It's fun to talk about this and remember things I may have forgotten.

Bill: The legendary Walter Cummins!

To listen to the complete interview, please visit *The Purpose Tree:* https://podcasts.apple.com

NOTES ON CONTRIBUTORS

Claire Bateman is the very first author published by Serving House Books with her chapbook *Coronology*. Among her full-length poetry books: *Locals* (Serving House, 2012), *Wonders of the Invisible World* (42 Miles Press, 2023), *Coronology* (Etruscan Press, 2010), *Scape* (New Issues Poetry & Prose, 2016), *Leap* (New Issues, 2005), *Clumsy* (New Issues Poetry & Prose, 2003), *At the Funeral of the Ether* (Ninety-Six Press, 1998). Her new fiction collection, *The Pillow Museum*, is forthcoming from FC2 in early 2025. She is also a visual artist.

Walter Cummins is the author of seven collections of short fiction, four essay collections, numerous other anthologies, and has had well over 100 stories published in international magazines and journals. He is the cofounder of Serving House Books. For more on his writing and career: www.waltercummins.com.

Eugene Datta is the author of the story collection *The Color of Noon* (Serving House, 2024). He is also the author of the poetry collection *Water & Wave* (Redhawk, 2024). His fiction and poetry have appeared in publications such as *Common Ground Review*, *The Dalhousie Review*, *Mantis*, *Hamilton Stone Review*, *The Bangalore Review*, and elsewhere. A recipient of the Stiftung Laurenz-Haus fellowship, he has held residencies at Ledig House International Writers' Colony, and Fundación Valparaíso. Eugene has worked as a newspaper journalist, a book reviewer, and an editor. Born and raised in India, he lives in Aachen, Germany.

Maria Mazziotti Gillan has published over two dozen books, including *What Blooms in Winter* (NYQ Books, 2016); *Ancestors' Song* (Bordighera Press, 2013); *The Silence in an Empty House* (NYQ Books, 2013); *Writing Poetry to Save Your Life* (MiroLand, Guernica Editions, 2013), among others. With her daughter Jennifer, she is co-editor of four anthologies. In 2017, Serving House produced a hardcover collection of her selected books paired with the photography of Mark Hillringhouse titled *Paterson Light and Shadow*. Visit her site at www.mariagillan.com

Barbara Froman received early training in music at the Juilliard School's preparatory division before going on to earn degrees in Music Composition at Ithaca College and Northwestern University. She was the Director of Mundelein College's Creative Writing Program, taught Literature and Creative Writing at National-Louis University, and acted as a consultant to National's graduate program in Written Communication. She is the author of published essays and poetry, has placed in screenwriting competitions, and was nominated for a Fringe First at the Edinburgh Fringe. She continues to compose music as well as work on a number of new writing projects. She is the author of the 2011 novel *Ghosts and Shadows* (Serving House Books).

Susan O'Neill spent a year as an Army nurse in the Viet Nam War. *Don't Mean Nothing* is a collection of inter-related short stories loosely based on this experience, updated for Serving House from its original Ballantine publication in 2001. She also has published a more recent collection of mostly-funny short nonfiction pieces with another house. Her short stories and essays have appeared in an eclectic variety of magazines, newspapers, anthologies, and internet and audio media, and she helped pioneer *Vestal Review* for Flash fiction, and co-edited it for 20 years. She now mostly mentors and edits emerging authors from her Brooklyn home.

Miriam Polli's debut novel *In a Vertigo of Silence* was named one of the Best Indie Books of 2015 by Kirkus Reviews. Her stories and poems have been published in commercial and literary magazines and are included in various anthologies. *Rosina* is her second novel and is forthcoming in 2025 by Serving House Books. Miriam is a native New Yorker and now lives in Virginia.

Diana Senechal is the 2011 winner of the Hiett Prize in the Humanities and the author of two books of nonfiction, *Republic of Noise* (2012) and *Mind over Memes* (2018), as well as numerous poems, stories, essays, songs, and translations. Her debut poetry collection *Solo Concert* is forthcoming in 2025 from Serving House Books. Her translations of the poetry of Tomas Venclova have been featured in two books *Winter Dialogue*, (1997) and *The Junction*, 2008). She is currently working on a book about the songwriting partnership of Tamás Cseh and Géza Bereményi. Since 2017 she has been teaching at the Varga Katalin Gimnázium in Szolnok; in 2024 she served as the president of the Association of Literary Scholars, Critics, and Writers. For more about her work, see her website dianasenechal.com.

Rita Signorelli-Pappas is the author of the forthcoming poetry collection *The Chameleon* (Serving House Books, 2025). Her poems have been published in *Poetry, Shenandoah, Southwest Review, Prairie Schooner, The Literary Review, Poet Lore, The Women's Review of Books, Southern Poetry Review, Notre Dame Review,* and other publications. Her previous two collections of poetry, *Satyr's Wife* (2010) and *Labyrinth* (2019), were both published by Serving House Books. She is a regular poetry reviewer for *World Literature Today,* and her fiction has appeared in *Helicon Nine, Italian Americana, Helicon Nine, Farmer's Market, Crosscurrents,* and *VIA*. Her short story, "Spirit Dreams" was nominated for a Pushcart Prize, and another received the fiction award in *Italian Americana.*

J.R. Solonche has published poetry in more than 400 magazines, journals, and anthologies since the early 70s. His titles with Serving House Books include *Selected Poems (2002-2021), Enjoy Yourself, Piano Music*, and *A Guide of the Perplexed.* He lives in the Hudson Valley.

Susan Tekulve is the author of the poetry book *Bodies of Light* (Serving House, 2024), which is her first full-length poetry collection. She is the author of *Second Shift: Essays* (Del Sol Press) and *In the Garden of Stone* (Hub City Press), winner of the South Carolina Novel Prize and a Gold IPPY Award. She is the author of two collections of stories: *Savage Pilgrims* (Serving House) and *My Mother's War* (Winnow Press). Her nonfiction, fiction, and poetry has appeared in *Denver Quarterly, The Georgia Review, The Louisville Review, Puerto del Sol, New Letters, Shenandoah,* and others. She has received scholarships from the Sewanee Writers' Conference and Bread Loaf Writers' Conference. She teaches in the BFA and MFA programs at Converse University.

Ronna Wineberg is the author of *Artifacts and Other Stories,* a collection of stories, winner of the 2004 American Fiction Award in short story fiction; *Nine Facts That Can Change Your Life,* a collection of stories, which received an Honorable Mention for the Eric Hoffer Book Award; *On Bittersweet Place,* her first novel, winner of the Shelf Unbound Best Indie Book Competition; and a debut collection, *Second Language,* winner of the New Rivers Press Many Voices Project Literary Competition, and chosen as the runner-up for the Reform Judaism Prize for Jewish Fiction. Her stories have appeared in *American Way, Colorado Review, Michigan Quarterly Review, South Dakota Review* and elsewhere, and been broadcast on National Public Radio. She is the recipient of a scholarship in fiction to the Bread Loaf Writers Conference and residencies to the Virginia Center for the Creative Arts and the Ragdale Foundation. She is the founding fiction editor of the *Bellevue Literary Review,* and lives in New York.

www.ingramcontent.com/pod-product-compliance
Lightning Source LLC
Chambersburg PA
CBHW021722190726
48289CB00008B/2642

* 9 7 8 1 9 4 7 1 7 5 7 9 2 *